The Observer's Pocket Series

HOUSE PLANTS

About the Book

This selection of house plants has been chosen to suit the environment of the modern home. 150 genera, taken from the author's larger work, *The Book of House Plants*, are concisely described, and beautifully illustrated in water colour by Joan Lupton. Dr Whitehead has purposely sought a balance between plants which can be grown indoors all the year round and those which are brought in for a short time when their floral colour and foliage are at their best. Exotic tropical plants, so suitable for central heating are included. In the Introduction helpful advice is given on how to match house plants to their surroundings and how to care for them. There is a glossary of technical terms and an index. A rewarding book for all who love to beautify and decorate their homes.

The Observer's Book of
HOUSE PLANTS

STANLEY B. WHITEHEAD

DESCRIBING 150 TYPES
ILLUSTRATED IN COLOUR

FREDERICK WARNE
LONDON

LIBRARY OF CONGRESS CATALOG
CARD NO 72-81145

ISBN 0 7232 1512 X

Printed in Great Britain by
Lowe & Brydone Printers Limited
Thetford, Norfolk
D6447.1280

CONTENTS

PREFACE

Houses make good homes for plants as well as for people, when rightly matched, and are the better for them. The objectives sought in this small book are the presentation of upwards of 200 of the most attractive and most suitable plants for indoors, and their culture, in simple, understandable and practical terms.

The selection has been made from my larger volume, *The Book of House Plants,* and purposely seeks a balance between plants which may be grown in the house all the year round—which some could claim to be the true house plants—and those which we may bring into the home for a lesser period when their beauty and floral colour are at their peak. It includes many of the more recently introduced exotic plants, so suitable for central heating, together with the traditionally popular.

150 different plants are portrayed in Miss Joan Lupton's exquisite water-colour paintings from life, and are readily identifiable by them.

Emphasis has naturally been placed upon the cultural needs for healthy, vigorous plants, but a guide to the chief diseases and pests and what can be done about them is included. With the hints on propagation it is hoped to add to the interest and pleasure that can be gained from growing house plants, especially for those without a garden.

Stanley B. Whitehead

INTRODUCTION

Plants Indoors

For the purpose of this book a house plant is defined as a plant having attractive characteristics of flower, foliage or form, which can adapt itself to the growing conditions found in a house for part of, or all, the year.

There are countless ways in which plants can be used indoors. On furniture pieces, such as a table or a sideboard, a single well-grown pot specimen gives warmth and invites interest. Windows are always attractive settings for plants. The harsh upright lines can be effectively framed with climbing plants, trained up a suitably firm framework, such as plastic-covered wire-mesh or strong wood trellis, which can be easily moved when necessary.

In rooms receiving ample light plants can stand free on floors or shelves within the room, or hung on walls. There is a wide variety of pot containers now available, made in plastic and pot, wickerwork and metal, colourful to match any existing decor. But it should be easy to lift pot and plant right out so that the plant may be watered by plunging on occasion, or for spraying, or for standing out of doors in warm weather.

An effective way of growing a collection of house plants is to place them in a trough made of wood, metal or plastic. Teak, Western Red Cedar or one of the African hardwoods is ideal for wooden troughs. Metal troughs may be made of galvanized steel, aluminium or one of its alloys, and old-fashioned or antique containers of copper, brass or zinc can be used as plant containers. On the inside, however, it is wise to paint such containers with moisture-resistant plastic or bituminous paint, to avoid oxidizing or sulphating reactions and their staining. Plastic troughs combine the advantages of a pleasing waterproof finish with a startling lightness in weight, and are labour-saving and easily handled.

Whatever type of trough is used a perforated false or double bottom should be provided for drainage.

When placing plants in troughs, they should be set in their pots packed around with a moist material such as horticultural peat or vermiculite, with their rims just below the edges of the trough. Where the trough has not a separate internal lining container, it is useful to line it with sheet polythene to hold the peat. This should be perforated at the base—easily done with a red-hot poker, a packing needle or pointed knife blade. The packing not only holds the plants firmly and provides a pleasing surface finish, but helps considerably to maintain equable growing conditions for the plants.

Artistic effects can be achieved by arrangements of the plants with different leaf shapes and variegations, and the contrast of forms—upright-growers being associated with the more bushy types, and trailers used to soften the edges of the trough outline. In juxtaposition, plants adjust their foliage to securing the maximum of light. Naturally, some plants grow more strongly than others, and when one threatens to swamp its neighbour, it is time to rearrange their setting. Wooden tubs of round, square or oval shape are splendid, and there is a range of deep bowl-shaped, cone-shaped and urn-shaped containers, made in porous concrete or red earthenware, that fit into metal tripods or supports. Many people find objects such as old brass or copper coal-scuttles adaptable. Groups of plants in their containers may be handled in decorative schemes much as pieces of furniture.

The placing of plants, while depending much upon personal taste and preference, must always take into account their needs for light, humidity and warmth.

Often, plants may serve a practical purpose in dividing room space, for which purpose climbing plants may be grown in a trough, with light metal-work trellis for support.

The modern plant room, or twentieth-century equivalent of the Victorian conservatory, may be planned as the extension of a living-room, projected into the garden. With large picture windows, preferably double-glazed, and a southern exposure to catch the maximum sun in winter, such a room enables the most exotic plants to be grown, and creates a garden effect indoors. The modern aluminium alloy type of Venetian blind and terylene curtaining can be used to moderate the fierceness of direct sunlight. Most house plants seldom require more than 60° to 65°F (15·5° to 18°C) minimum night temperature, and many are healthy with less. The floor of the plant room should be of tiles or mosaic so that plants can be syringed freely and cleaning may be easy. Ventilation can be provided very effectively by means of an extractor fan or louvred top-lights to the windows. In such a room foliage plants can attain their full growth, and show their true qualities. It is often practical to grow them in sunken troughs or beds near the windows, though these should be lined with inner containers to facilitate soil changes when necessary.

Another way is to build out a deep bay or alcove window from an existing room, and make this a feature for house plants.

A third way of growing plants indoors is in an enclosed plant case or cabinet where growing conditions can be closely controlled by artificial means. The cabinets are made with internal heating and lighting, and ventilation and humidity can be easily regulated. The plants may be grown in their pots on trays, filled with gravel or small pebbles, and arranged in tiers in the cabinet, with each tier or shelf of plants being illuminated by means of fluorescent light tubes, which give sufficient light for plants to be grown independently of any natural daylight reaching them; indeed some plants flower more readily and for longer periods under fluorescent light tubes than under natural light, although the latter may be of somewhat higher intensity. Of the standard types of fluorescent tubes, the 'white', 'warm white' and 'daylight' kinds are all successful with plants, though the 'warm white' are preferable for flowering plants, and the others most effective for purely foliage plants. Since they run at cooler temperatures than the tungsten filament lamps, they can be used at distance of only 10 to 11 in. from the foliage of plants; in some cases even more closely. Heating can be controlled thermostatically, and lighting by time switch, and access to the plants for watering and attention is simply arranged by sliding glass panels.

Choosing House Plants

When choosing house plants, we cannot simply set out fancy free and select plants that appeal to us purely on aesthetic grounds. Choice must necessarily be tempered by the conditions we can offer plants in the home for their health and growth in terms of light, temperature, humidity and atmosphere. The provision of a good rooting medium or compost, proper watering, feeding, and disease- and pest-preventing care are also highly important.

Plants that are usually grown in the home may be divided into three groups.

1 **Temporary house plants** These consist of (a) bulbous or cormus plants, such as hyacinth, daffodil and tulip, and (b) herbs such as *Cineraria*, *Calceolaria*, and tender perennials and annuals brought into the home largely because of their lengthy flowering period, and then discarded.

Bulbous and Cormous Plants for the House

Kind	Planting time	Flower colour	When in bloom in the home
Crocus sp.	Sept–Oct	Blue, white yellow	Feb–Mar
Hyacinths, Dutch	Aug	All colours	Jan–Apl
Hyacinths, Roman	Aug	White	Dec–Jan
Narcissi	Aug–Sept	Yellow, white	Feb–Apl
Narcissus, 'Paper White'	Aug–Sept	White	Dec–Jan
Narcissus, 'Soleil d'Or'	Aug–Sept	Yellow	Dec–Jan
Tulipa sp.	Sept–Nov	Various	Mar–May

The plants that are grown anew each year and brought into the house for their flowering period are usually reared under glass in heated greenhouses, and introduced at the point of bloom. Such plants include the herbaceous *Calceolaria*, the Slipper Flower; *Campanula pyramidalis*, the Chimney Bell-flower; *Chrysanthemum frutescens*; *Cineraria* (*Senecio cruentus* hybrids); *Francoa ramosa*, Bridal Wreath; *Impatiens balsamina*, Balsam; and *Ionopsidium acaule*.

2 **Perennial plants grown as house plants during their flowering periods, and later rested out of doors or under glass** This group consists of (a) bulbous, cormous or rhizomatous plants, which, with good cultured care, can be grown to flower in the house year after year, and (b) shrubs, deciduous and evergreen.

Plants grown from bulbs, corms or rhizomes include *Achimenes* hybrids; *Amaryllis belladonna*, the Daffodil Lily; Begonias; *Clivia miniata*, Caffre Lily; *Cyclamen persicum*; *Gesneria cardinalis*; *Haemanthus katherinae*, Blood Flower; *Hippeastrum* hybrids, Barbados Lily; *Incarvillea delavayi*; *Nerine sarniensis*, Guernsey Lily;

Sinningia sp., *Gloxinia*; and *Vallota speciosa*, Scarborough Lily.

The shrubs chosen for flowering house plants are half-hardy. They are often placed out of doors for the frost-free months, June to September, and then brought into the house again for another season of flowering. They include *Acacia* sp., often called Mimosa; *Erica* sp., Heaths; *Epacris impressa*, Australian Heaths; *Hydrangea macrophylla*; *Iochroma lanceolata*; *Rhododendron obtusum* varieties, Kurume Azaleas; *Rhododendron simsii*, Indian Azaleas; *Solanum* sp., Jerusalem Cherry; *Sparmannia africana*, African Hemp; and shrubby forms of *Pelargonium*.

3 **Permanent house plants** These are perennial plants, mostly evergreen, that can be grown in the house year after year. They can only succeed permanently where room conditions approximate to those of their native habitat. Plants with an ability to thrive in shade, for instance, are usually drawn from the undergrowth of woods and forests or shaded ravines and valleys. Others with an ability to thrive under fluctuating conditions of dryness and moisture or wide variations in temperature are drawn from regions of weather fluctuations or extremes, such as deserts.

House plants should be chosen to suit the rooms and conditions under which they are to grow. Here are some selective lists of house plants to grow under the conditions described.

Easily-grown house plants These consist of hardy plants for indoors, capable of thriving in conditions of fluctuating temperatures, and of withstanding a certain amount of neglect in watering, feeding and change of soil compost, though none of these things is advocated as a regular practice.

Aspidistra lurida	x *Fatshedera lizei*
Chlorophytum elatum	*Fatsia japonica*
Cissus antarctica	*Ficus elastica*

Francoa ramosa
Guzmania monostachya
Haworthia attenuata
Haworthia chalwinii
Hedera helix and vars.
Philodendron scandens
Pilea cadierei
Rebutia deminuta, R. grandiflora
Rhoicissus rhomboidea
Sansevieria trifasciata
Saxifraga stolonifera
Schefflera actinophylla
Sygonium podophyllum
Tradescantia fluminensis and vars.
Vriesia splendens
Zebrina pendula and vars.
Zygocactus truncatus

Easy plants for heated rooms (minimum winter temperature of 50° to 55°F (10° to 12°C). These plants are more tender and need more consistent watering and attention to their individual needs. They do well under cool greenhouse conditions.

Adiantum capillus-veneris
Aloe variegata
Anthurium scherzerianum
Asplenium nidus
Begonias, fibrous-rooted
Begonia semperflorens
Beleperone guttata
Bilbergia nutans
Coffea arabica
Cordyline terminalis
Crassula arborescens
Crassula falcata
Crassula lactea
Davallia canariensis
Drosera binnata, D. capensis
Dryopteris sieboldii
Echeveria sp.
Echinocactus horizonthalonius
Echinocereus pectinatus
Epiphyllum ackermannii
Euphorbia meloformis
Euphorbia splendens
Ficus benjamina
Hoya carnosa
Maranta leuconeura
Monstera deliciosa and vars.
Nephrolepsis exaltata
Nertera granadensis
Nidularium sp.
Opuntia fragilis
Pandanus sp. (Screw Pines)
Pelargonium sp.
Peperomia caperata
Peperomia hederifolia
Peperomia sandersii
Philodendron bipinnatifidum
Philodendron elegans
Philodendron erubescens
Philodendron lacineatum

13

Philodendron melano-
chrysum
Philodendron sagittifolium
Philodendron wendlandii
Scindapsus aureus and
vars.

Scindapsus picta var.
argyraeus
Sedum sieboldii, S. stahlii
Spathiphyllum wallisii
Syngonium vellozianum

Delicate plants for heated rooms (minimum winter temperature of 56°F (12° to 15·5°C). These are plants that require a degree of skill to keep them growing perennially, under conditions of even, rather high temperatures, and controlled humidity; what gardeners refer to as stove or hothouse conditions.

Aphelandra squarrosa
Begonia boweri
Begonia 'Lorraine' hybrids
Begonia masoniana
Begonia rex and vars.
Caladium sp.
Calathea sp.
Codiaeum variegatum
(Croton)
Dieffenbachia sp.

Dizygotheca elegantissima
Dracaena godseffiana and
vars.
Fittonia argyroneura, F.
verschaffeltii
Maranta makoyana
Philodendron verrucosum
Saintpaulia ionantha and
vars.

The Management of House Plants

Plants in the house can continue to live only where they receive the minimum of light, air, warmth, humidity and food to which they have become adjusted in their evolution. Their likes and dislikes have to be considered according to their type and origins, and according to their growth.

Light All green plants respond to light since it regulates their growth. The green pigment of leaves and stems (chlorophyll) absorbs certain light rays and converts them into the energy which sparks the process known as photosynthesis. In this process carbon dioxide is taken from the air and combined with water from the soil to form sugars (carbohydrates), which may in turn be converted into starches and stored in the tissues. These carbohydrates provide food-energy for other essential growth processes and build up the substance of the plant.

Up to a certain point, the more light a plant receives in intensity and duration, the greater the rate of photosynthesis, and the greater the need for water, warmth and nutrients to support the process. The level at which the rate of photosynthesis virtually ceases to increase varies with the type of plant and also with the temperature. Too much light, especially direct sunlight, overtaxes the plant and is apt to lead to wilting and scorching. Too little forces weak, pallid growth, and encourages vegetative growth at the expense of flowering.

Broadly, the richer and deeper the green, the more able is the plant to absorb light, and the more adaptable it is to shade. Pale colouring and variegation in leaves, however, mean that less chlorophyll is present, and such plants need ample light to prosper and retain their ornamental appeal. Plants that flower need ample light before and during flowering when they are making active growth, and should therefore be given well-lighted positions in rooms. Most cacti and succulents also need ample sun. The tendency of plants to grow towards the source of light can be corrected to some extent by turning the plants round, gradually and regularly rather than abruptly.

The rate of photosynthesis is affected by the temperature in which a plant is grown. This means that light and heat should be in proportion to one another. Warmth increases the rate at which chemical changes go forward within the plant, and therefore the rate of photosynthesis. The higher the temperature, within reason, the more light a plant needs and can use. But light, not heat, is the critical factor. It is the low light intensity of winter, rather than the low temperature, that limits the growth of plants during the winter months.

Light intensity in rooms is affected by their colour schemes, and the use of white, cream or pastel-hued walls and ceilings is helpful because of the greater amount of light they reflect. Blacks, blues and reds, however, are light absorbent and poor backgrounds for plants.

In the home the normal space lighting by means of tungsten filament lamp bulbs or low pressure fluorescent tubes does not greatly affect the growth of house plants, but suitably arranged to irradiate the plants directly, fluorescent tubes can assist flowering of such plants as South African Violets, and have formative effects upon the plants.

Temperature All plants have a range of temperatures within which they grow best, and a somewhat wider range within which they can still grow and remain alive. The temperature limits of this growth-range vary for different plants, largely according to their native origins. A plant will not necessarily die if subjected temporarily to temperatures outside its growth-range, but if it is to succeed as a house plant, it must have the degree of warmth conducive to its optimum preformance.

The critical temperature is that prevailing at night, in cold weather. Since photosynthesis does not take place in darkness, the plant is less active and the temperature at night can, and should, fall by some degrees, providing that it does not fall below the minimum tolerated by the type of plant. When rooms are kept at a high or constant temperature it is advantageous to move plants to cooler conditions at night.

Within the range of tolerated temperatures, the higher this is, the more active the plant, and the more moisture it uses and transpires. Consequently, plants in heated rooms need more attention.

Humidity The greatest danger to plants in heated confinement is dryness of the atmosphere. Apart from the excessive transpiration of moisture from the leaves and top growth of a plant that this causes, moisture also evaporates quickly from the soil and pots and roots of the plant. Correction by extra watering seldom works, for the plant cannot absorb the extra moisture readily. The soil becomes over-wet and the roots rot, while the leaves begin to brown at the edges, shrivel and fall. This can be avoided by creating an atmosphere of some humidity about the plant: by standing the plants in their pots on large saucers or trays holding gravel, shingle or pebbles which are kept moist with water up to half their depth; by placing a pot in a larger container, filling the space between with packed moist sphagum moss, or moist peat or some water-holding medium. The steady evaporation thus provides the humidity that most house plants naturally appreciate. In cold weather it is helpful to moisten the absorbent material with very hot water. Atmospheric dryness can also be offset by mist-spraying the foliage on sunny days and in warm weather, so that the foliage is surface-dry by night.

Ventilation Plants need what gardeners call a buoyant atmosphere, in which the air is warm, humid, yet always moving, avoiding the stagnancy which invites disease and certain pests. It is usually possible, and a good plan, to open windows on sunny days in the warmer midday hours, even in winter, sufficiently long to induce a change of air.

Draughts at any time are deadly to plants, not so much because of their physical force, but because they accentuate conditions accompanying them. When a plant must be placed in a known draughty position for its decorative merits it is often possible to improve matters by placing a glass or a lattice screen between it

and the direction of the draught, preferably at an angle
to deflect the air current.

Water Throughout their growth water is a constant,
though not necessarily a regular, need of all plants.
They need it to provide hydrogen and oxygen to unite
with the carbon dioxide of air in the photosynthesis of
carbohydrates; they need it as the solvent and carrier
of nutrients from root to leaf; and it constitutes at
least 80 per cent, often more, of their substance.

Plants get their water from the rooting medium in
which they grow. The amount they need varies considerably according to their kind, the stage of the
growth cycle they are in, and environmental conditions.

Plants need water most when in active growth, and
their need is roughly proportional to their transpiring
leaf, or top growth, surface area. Evergreens are in
active growth all the year round, by virtue of retaining
their leaves. Evergreens of a tropical origin, such as a
rain forest, are more or less in continuous growth, and
the dormant period, more properly termed the rest
period, may only be short. The growth of other plants
may be more sharply affected by a native habitat
governed by alternating wet and dry seasons. Broadly
speaking, a plant needs increasing supplies of water as
it waxes in growth, decreasing as it wanes, and little
or none during its dormant or rest period.

Day-to-day water requirements, however, are in-
fluenced by several factors. The nature of the rooting
medium and its moisture-holding capacity, and the
size and nature of the pot affect the frequency of watering. Temperature, degree of exposure to light and
shade, and the humidity of the surrounding atmosphere all play a part in determining the amount of
water a plant can use—and therefore needs. The
watering of house plants calls for skill and intelligence,
rather than for hit-and-miss methods.

On the whole, plants are better constituted to withstand water shortages than water excesses, and when in doubt it is wiser to err on the side of too little than too much. The traditional test is to rap a pot sharply with a wooden stick or hammer or flick it with a thumb and listen to the sound. If the pot gives a ringing sound it is considered that the soil is well aerated and water is needed. If it gives a dull sound it is considered that the soil is moist enough. More accurate readings of the water state of the soil can be obtained by the use of instruments, such as a tensiometer, which measure the moisture content of the soil.

Newly potted plants and plants just starting into new growth may be efficiently watered by immersing the pots to their soil level in a bath of water and letting the soil absorb the water through the drainage holes and pot walls until the surface glistens. The pot must then be stood to drain immediately, and not placed in its growing position until the excess water has drained through.

This immersion technique is also useful in watering plants that do best when their mass roots are densely matted and pot-bound, such as palms and hydrangeas, and for plants that are sensitive to moisture on their crown leaves. After this initial soaking, plants should be given no more water until active growth in new buds and unfurling leaves is seen. Thereafter water should be supplied whenever needed, increasing in quantity and frequency with growth and warm seasonable growing conditions.

The more intense the light and the higher the temperature, the more water a plant needs. At lower temperatures and in shaded surroundings, transpiration and photosynthesis go on more slowly and less water is needed. Then it should be obvious that a plant in a small pot will need more frequent watering than one in a larger pot with its greater capacity. The fact that clay pots, being porous, absorb and lose moisture more readily than plastic pots must also be borne in mind.

Although rain water, stream water, well water, or soft water is preferable, it is not essential. The water supply available through the tap is satisfactory, though hard or lime-containing water will have to be avoided for the watering of Rhododendrons (Azaleas) and lime-intolerant plants. Stagnant water is best avoided as it is almost certain to contain algae and cause a greening of the soil surface.

After watering, the surplus water should be allowed to drain through before the pot is replaced on its saucer or in its container. It is slowly fatal to let pots stand in water.

Food Since plants in pots have only a limited volume of soil to exploit for the nutrients they need, they benefit from additional feeding. The purpose of feeding, however, is to supplement the nutrient resources of the soil, which itself should be well-constituted and provided with a correct balance of basic fertilizer materials.

Supplementary feeding should be given only to plants that are established and in active growth. A newly re-potted plant needs nothing but water until it has developed an active rooting system. Sick plants seldom benefit from supplementary feeding, except where the trouble is caused by a nutrient deficiency, since they cannot make much use of the nutrients so provided. Again, no feeding should be attempted when a plant is dormant or resting.

House plants should be fed from the time that growth is well forward to the time that they begin to mature the current year's growth and no further new leaves are being budded or emerging. In the case of most plants this is roughly from late March to October, and feeding should stop a little before watering is restricted and finished.

There are two general methods of feeding: (1) by

using the fertilizer in prepared dry powdered or crystalline form or as a compressed tablet, sprinkled on, or inserted in the soil and allowed to dissolve in subsequent waterings; this should be done once every three or four weeks; (2) by using liquid solutions of fertilizers; once every ten to fourteen days.

Liquid fertilizers act more quickly, and it is sometimes advantageous to wet plant foliage with them, since nutrients may be absorbed by the leaves. They must, however, be used in proper dilution, since strong solutions are likely to scorch and damage the leaves. There are several proprietary products put up in liquid form; or the John Innes Liquid Feed—fifteen parts by weight ammonium sulphate, two and three-quarter parts potassium nitrate, and two and a quarter parts mono-ammonium phosphate, used at $\frac{1}{4}$ oz to $\frac{1}{2}$ oz per gallon of water—can be made up and used freshly dissolved.

Cleaning of plants Plants and their foliage in the home inevitably collect dust which impairs leaf function in photosynthesis and respiration, and periodically should be removed by sponging or spraying. A little milk added to the water imparts a sheen to the leaves that is pleasing.

Fine-leaved plants can be cleansed by close-up spraying with a mist sprayer, but plants with hairy or downy leaves, and cacti and succulents can be more effectively freed of dust with a fine camel-hair brush. In warm weather, when rain falls gently without wind, plants may be stood out of doors for an hour or two in summer.

Fallen foliage and dying flowers need to be promptly removed and the surface soil lightly pricked over, and moss and liverwort growth removed.

Potting and re-potting The living functions of perennial plants never cease, but there is a time in their annual cycle when they are at their lowest ebb, and the plants enjoy dormancy or a rest period. This rest period usually follows flowering and fruiting. In some plants it is of short duration, as in most leafy evergreens. In others, such as cacti, it may last for months.

As plants begin to awaken from their rest period, budding new leaves, stems and root extensions, it is time to pot the new and re-pot the older and established plants. In the case of most house plants this opportunity comes in early spring, from late February to late May, though bulbous, cormous and rhizomatous plants may be potted in summer or autumn.

Whether a young plant is being potted or an older established plant is being re-potted, the sequence of operations is similar. The plant itself should be in soil on the dry side, not freshly watered, so that it can be easily dislodged from its present pot and will integrate with the new soil more readily.

A clean pot is essential. Pots greened from former use should be steeped in a bath of potassium permanganate ($\frac{1}{2}$ oz per gallon of water) overnight. The drainage hole should be covered with a crock (pieces of broken plant pot) or two, a disc of perforated zinc or fine nylon mesh, and then enough soil compost added so that with the plant resting on it, it is planted at the correct depth. Soil is then added around the sides of the plant, pressed firmly down with fingers and thumbs until the roots are covered. The final topping should finish sufficiently below the rim of the pot to allow for watering.

When established plants are re-potted some of the old soil should be teased out from among the roots and some of the top-soil removed. Long straggling roots that have wrapped themselves round the wall of the pot may be thinned out, and very coarse roots with few root fibres trimmed. Young plants, growing vigorously, usually need to be potted on into a one-size larger pot annually or biennially, according to vigour. Well-established pot plants which have been potted into adequate size pots only need re-potting every third or fourth year, given a good compost that remains open and porous, and good culture.

After potting, the plant should be well watered, and then given no more water until it is showing signs of new growth and kept in partial shade until growth becomes stiff and turgid, a light mist spraying being given if the atmosphere is dry.

Soil mixtures and composts   The rooting medium in which house plants grown in pots are expected to flourish must be properly constituted. Today research has led to the development of standardized formulae.

In Britain the formulae tested and evolved at the John Innes Horticultural Institution, and known as the John Innes Composts, may be bought ready mixed from any good nurseryman or horticultural sundriesman, or made up at home by the gardener. The basic formulae are as follows:

John Innes Seed Compost (usually abbreviated as JIS)

Two parts by volume medium loam, sterilized

One part by volume horticultural sedge or sphagnum moss peat

One part by volume coarse sand

Plus per bushel (8 gal)

$\frac{3}{4}$ oz ground chalk or limestone or whiting

$1\frac{1}{2}$ oz superphosphate (16-18 per cent P_2O_5).

This formula is suitable for raising house plants from seed, and also for growing cuttings.

John Innes Potting Compost (JIP)

Seven parts by volume medium loam, sterilized

Three parts by volume horticultural sedge or sphagnum moss peat

Two parts by volume coarse sand

Plus per bushel (8 gal)

$\frac{3}{4}$ oz ground chalk or limestone or whiting

4 oz. John Innes Base (JIB) Fertilizer

The John Innes Base Fertilizer may be bought ready mixed, or made up to the formula of two parts by weight hoof and horn meal, two parts superphosphate (16-18 per cent P_2O_5) and one part sulphate of potash (48-50 per cent K_2O).

Made up to this formula, the potting compost is known as JIP No. 1, and is chiefly advised for the first potting-on of young plants, and for the pot-growth of the majority of succulents.

For a second potting-on of plants into 5- or 6-in. pots, a richer compost is used, known as JIP No. 2, to the same basic formula but with the double quantity of ground chalk or limestone and JIB Fertilizer. For plants in larger pots, a richer compost still, JIP No. 3, is needed, in which the quantity of ground chalk and JIB Fertilizer is trebled.

The John Innes Composts are suitable for the majority of house plants, though for plants which are intolerant of lime (calcifuge), the ground chalk or limestone should be left out.

Many house plants grow naturally where decaying leaves and plant remains accumulate, and therefore appreciate a more humus-containing rooting medium. This can be most satisfactorily arranged by adding one to two parts, by volume, of sifted oak or beech leaf-mould to John Innes Compost. Plants of the Araceae, Begoniaceae, Piperaceae, Marantaceae families, and the *Cordyline* and *Dracaena* genera of the Liliaceae, are those which benefit.

Epiphytic plants, particularly those of the Bromeliaceae family, require little or no soil in the compost and can be well grown in a mixture of:

Four parts by volume sifted leaf-mould
Two parts by volume sphagnum moss peat
One part by volume Osmunda fibre
One part by volume coarse sand
Plus per bushel
4 oz JIB Fertilizer, 2 oz crushed charcoal.

Cacti and succulent plants need a soil mixture that drains freely without drying out too quickly. For those grown as house plants JIP No. 1 compost, plus two parts of sand and one of limestone grit, or a mixture of equal parts by volume of medium loam, horticultural peat and coarse sand, with half a part of limestone grit, and 4 oz. bone-meal per bushel, may be used.

In recent years, soil-less composts, made up of moss peat and sand, plus fertilizers and lime to provide the correct nutrient balance, are increasingly used, and available ready mixed, under proprietary names.

The latest development is to grow exotic plants in water by hydroculture. The plants are grown with their roots in a special medium of fired, inert clay granules or leca, aerated in structure, in net or slatted pots, placed inside decorative containers. A nutrient solution is added to a float indicated level, which is then maintained by adding water as needed. Every six months a special phial of nutrients is added, based on an ion exchange resin, to maintain the correct nutrient balance. Plants grow excellently, and their care is simplified.

Pots and containers for house plants Plants can be grown in a variety of pots and containers.

The clay pot is widely used, despite its weight and susceptibility to breakage. For re-use, clay pots need soaking for at least twenty-four hours in water to which potassium permanganate ($\frac{1}{4}$ oz per gallon) or domestic bleach solution of an algaecide has been added, and then washing.

Plastic pots combine lightness of weight with excellent maintenance of growing conditions in that the soil is kept at a more even temperature and with a slower rate of moisture evaporation. The plastic pot is non-porous and much easier to clean for re-use.

Another type of pot is made of long-fibred sphagnum moss peat and wood fibre. Light in weight, relatively strong and durable, it is designed to encourage the growth of roots out to, and through, the pot walls.

Pruning and training In the interest of shapeliness house plants often need pruning. When it is desired to remove weak, disorderly shoot growth or to cut back a plant it should be done in the latter half of spring, cutting the growth right out at its base or junction with an older stem, or to just above the good bud or leaf from which new growth is desired.

In the case of climbing plants and evergreens, bushy growth can be encouraged by a simple process of 'stopping' or pinching out the growing tips of shoots just above a leaf. Ivies and climbing Philodendrons can be treated in this way. Some house plants are really trees and may need curtailment in time, such as *Ficus elastica* and *Grevillea robusta*, in which case they can be induced to branch by being shortened in spring.

In the case of flowering plants, those that form their buds on new growth each year, such as *Sparmannia africana*, benefit from being pruned quite hard in spring, but those which form their buds on older growth need very little pruning beyond the occasional cutting back of a shoot to keep a shapely appearance.

Climbing foliage plants such as *Cissus* and trailing plants such as *Tradescantia* may be kept neat by having their growing points stopped from time to time during the growing season.

Some plants may tend to bleed after being cut, and cuts should be dressed with a little sulphur paste, powdered charcoal or a proprietary antiseptic (Arbrex).

Tall-growing plants will need the support of stakes, and even robust shrubs such as Hydrangeas benefit from supports given to their branches, since growth indoors is always softer and less firm than when it is tested and hardened by winds outside. Canes are excellent for this purpose, and split cane can be used for smaller plants. Climbing plants used to decorate large surfaces such as walls may be trained up light trellis, or a network of wire or plastic mesh, but if the plants are not to interfere with domestic cleaning, the framework or support should be integral with the pot and move with it. In training plants around windows, however, it may be necessary to attach some support to the wall or woodwork, but it is best to make this removable rather than permanently attached.

Propagating House Plants

Plants reproduce themselves (a) sexually by seeds, and (b) asexually by vegetative propagation of their parts, Plants from seeds manifest the genetical characteristics of their parentage. The vegetative propagation of a plant makes it possible for us to reproduce it identically.

From seeds To germinate readily, seeds need only three things—air, moisture and warmth. Not until the seedlings are showing growth above the soil and roots are being put forth are light and food essential.

For most of the house plants that can be grown from seed, the John Innes Seed Compost (JIS), or a soil-less seed compost is suitable. The sifted compost should be firmed and levelled in seed trays or shallow clay seed pans (with drainage holes crocked or covered with a piece of perforated zinc) and watered thoroughly with a fine spray. It is then ready for sowing.

A sensible rule is to sow at a depth equal to twice the seed's biggest diameter. Nevertheless, the seeds of many house plants are very small and such seeds need no more than a gentle pressing into the surface of the seed compost, or to be lightly covered with a sifting of sand. The seeds may be sown broadcast or in rows, thinly. The seed container should then be covered closely with a sheet of glass or more simply and safely by slipping the whole seed tray or pan into a polythene bag, drawn taut at the top and fastened with a rubber band or Sellotape. A sheet of kraft paper on top of the polythene will give the seeds darkness.

Then the seeds must be given soil warmth or bottom heat, as it is termed. All seeds germinate best at temperatures slightly higher than the plant's need for growth. Broadly speaking, seeds of plants from temperate climes need a temperature of 60° to 65°F (15·5° to 18°C), and those of semi-tropical and tropical habitats 70° to 80°F (21° to 26·5°C). Although it is often possible to germinate in the airing cupboard or on the window-sill of a heated room, the best place to do it is in a small propagating frame or unit. Self-contained units of this type are on the market. In a greenhouse a propagating frame can be used over a source of heat.

As soon as the seedlings are of a size that they can be easily moved with a small lifting fork and fingers they should be transplanted to small pots—the peat-wood fibre pots are ideal for this purpose—in a richer soil compost such as John Innes Potting Compost No. 1 (see page 23), and grown on under slightly cooler conditions until of a size suitable for potting-on again.

Vegetative propagation This consists of taking a part of a living plant with active, growing but undifferentiated cells that can be induced to form roots and make top growth and so form a separate plant. It is important to start with healthy, vigorous and well-grown stock. The chief ways of propagating house plants vegetatively are:

Division The plant should be knocked out of its pot, the roots gently teased apart so that pieces, each with a separate stem, leaf or crown, can be singled out and removed with roots attached. Severance should be done with a clean sharp knife or razor-blade. Each division is potted as a separate plant in an appropriate size of pot, using a good growing compost, firmed, watered, and placed in a propagating frame with light shade, until growing strongly.

Offsets Some plants form short stems or runners bending upward from their base with rosettes or clusters of leaves at their tips, which are called offsets.

These offsets may be detached in spring, inserted firmly in a soil compost suitable for the species in separate pots and rooted in warm, humid conditions. The Bromeliads—*Aechmea*, *Billbergia*, *Nidularium* and *Vriesia*—are stemless plants of rosette growth, propagated in this way. *Aloe*, *Gasteria*, *Haworthia*, and *Sedum* may be propagated similarly.

Offsets are also produced by bulbous plants in the shape of smaller daughter bulbs at the side of the original bulb. These may be detached when the annual growth cycle is completed and potted separately for growing on.

Layers A layer is a shoot or stem induced to root and so form a separate plant while still attached to the parent plant. There are two methods—soil-layering and air-layering.

Soil-layering is useful chiefly for plants that produce stolons or runners, after the manner of strawberries, with small plantlets on them, such as *Chlorophytum elatum*, the plantlets being inserted in JIP compost in small pots placed beside the parent plant and firmed and pegged down. They are not severed until rooted. *Saxifraga sarmentosa* and *Tolmeia menziesii* may be propagated similarly.

Air-layering is practised on shoots that cannot be bent down easily, and is a useful way of propagating overgrown plants, such as *Ficus elastica*, *Monstera*, *Fatsia japonica*, and *Grevillea robusta*. A narrow ring of bark is removed just below a suitably placed bud on the stem, or a slanting upward cut made half-way through the stem, and a little sphagnum moss inserted to keep it open. Any leaves are detached, and the area may be treated with a root-inducing 'hormone' powder or solution. A large handful of sphagnum moss, well moistened with a dilute solution of the root-inducing hormone preparation, is then wrapped around the stem to encase the prepared cut, and itself enclosed in a polythene 'sleeve', tied below and above with tape, and sealed. When white roots can be seen penetrating freely through the moss, the layer can be severed, the polythene removed, and the rooted portion carefully potted and then grown on as a newly-potted plant.

Cuttings Parts of a living plant severed from it to be rooted and grown as separate but identical specimens are termed cuttings. They may be rooted in plain, moist, coarse sand, fine vermiculite, or well-chopped sphagnum moss, but once the roots are developing well, they need to be transferred to richer compost, such as JIP No. 1. It is more practical to root cuttings in a balanced soil compost such as JIS or JIP No. 1.

To root a few cuttings, a plant pot or deep seed pan can be used, and a close atmosphere assured by fitting a glass jar or bell-glass, or a polythene bag on a simple frame on top. For more serious work a propagating case or box is most useful; this can consist of a strong wood box, 4 to 5 in. deep, with ½-in. drainage holes in the base, spaced about 4 in. apart; with a sheet of glass, heavy gauge polythene or perspex for a cover-lid. Alternatively a box can be made to take a low-barn cloche, sealed at the ends with pieces of glass cut to fit. Such containers, however, need to be placed in a warm place or over a source of gentle bottom heat.

Cuttings of house plants usually consist of stem or leaf cuttings, taken when the plants are in active growth, in spring, summer or autumn.

Stem cuttings are usually taken from the ends of young soft-wood, robust shoots in active growth, cut cleanly with a razor-blade or sharp knife, between the nodes (or leaves). In the case of very soft-tissued plants such as Pelargoniums ('Geraniums') and succulents, the cuttings should be allowed to lie for a few hours to let the cut surface dry off, or should be dipped in powdered charcoal. The cuttings should be stripped of their lower leaves, inserted and firmed in the rooting medium for two-thirds to one-half their length, and lightly sprayed with water before being covered with glass and a sheet of newspaper in their container.

Stem cuttings may also be taken from mature and harder shoots in the case of such plants as *Cissus, Hedera, Fatshedera* and *Ficus.* These are cut in short lengths of about 1 in., each with a leaf attached, and inserted upright in the soil up to the leaf axil. The cut ends should be sprinkled with, or dipped in, powdered charcoal to check bleeding.

Cuttings of Philodendrons, *Dracaena, Dieffenbachia* and *Hoya* can be similarly sectioned into inch lengths, but the leaf is then removed, and the section laid horizontally on the rooting medium, and firmed. Roots 'strike' from the slight swelling on the underside.

Cuttings consisting of short lateral shoots, detached with a slight 'heel' of older wood at their junction with a larger stem, may be taken from the shrubs such as *Solanum capsicastrum,* stripped of their lower leaves and inserted firmly in the rooting medium.

Leaf cuttings are taken for the propagation of fleshy-leaved plants, succulents and certain cacti. One method is to detach a mature adult leaf with stalk from the parent plant, and insert it upright in the rooting medium with the blade of the leaf just above the surface. African Violet (*Sainpaulia*), Gloxinias, *Gesneria, Peperomia* and *Tolmiea* may be propagated by this method. Baby plants develop at the base of the stalks.

The leaves of African Violet and *Tolmiea* may be rooted in water. A glass jar is partly filled with water, covered with stout paper in which holes are made so that the leaf stalks can be inserted to be immersed in the water below; when the little plantlets appear they are potted-on.

Well-grown leaves of succulents carefully detached from the plant and laid on a rooting medium with the plant end lightly firmed in contact with the soil, form young plants readily. In the case of *Sanseviera* the leaf blades can be cut into 2- to 3-in. lengths. These succulent leaves are best left to dry off and callus for a day or two before being planted.

The second way of propagating by leaf cuttings is used for large leaves with prominent veins, especially *Begonia rex*. A firm mature leaf with an inch of stalk is taken in spring, and the main veins cut through just below where they divide on the underside, using a razor-blade. The leaf is then laid right side up on the surface of the rooting medium anchored flat with the help of small stones or small bent pins over the main veins. The box should be covered with a pane of glass, wiped free of moisture twice a day. In about six weeks, small plantlets grow from the cuts, and these should be cut out for potting-on. The leaves of *Peperomia sandersii* may be cut in two, and each half inserted vertically in the same way.

Ferns can often be propagated by placing short lengths of spore-bearing fronds, spore-side down, on the surface of a seed pan to spore and then germinate and grow into new plants.

Keeping House Plants Healthy

In the protected and warm environment of a house, plants make rather softer tissue growth and are thus more susceptible to neglect, infections and infestations. Insufficient light causes drawn elongated growth, leggy weak stems and pale etiolated foliage. Too much light often causes wilting, even with plants known to be adequately watered.

Lack of fresh air impairs plant function. There should therefore be a current of air consistent with a gentle change of the atmosphere in rooms where plants are grown.

Too high a temperature causes wilting and exhaustion, and flowering to be curtailed. Too low temperatures retard growth.

Correct watering is more important to the healthy and successful growth of house plants than any other single factor. A sensible policy is to water regularly, but vary the amount according to temperature and light conditions, giving less in dull, cool periods than in periods of heat and much sun.

It is necessary to prick the surface soil from time to time to allow for aeration and the movement of air and water vapour out of, as well as into, the rooting medium.

The growth of algae, mosses, liverworts, and lichens on the soil in pots may not directly impair the growth and health of the house plants, but it does compete for air, moisture and nutrients, as well as being aesthetically undesirable. It is best removed, and replaced with a mulch of fresh compost; a crystal or two of potassium permanganate in the water when watering will discourage it.

Diseases and their control House plants grown under healthy indoor conditions are not prone to fungus diseases.

Mildews, characterized by a white powdery film on the leaves and aerial parts of a plant, may occur in late summer or autumn, and call for a dinocap or thiram fungicidal dust or spray for control.

Grey Mould, caused by the fungus *Botrytis cinerea*, shows as a blackish rot and greyish fluffy growth on plants; the infected part should be cut out and the plant sprayed with a benomyl, captan, or copper fungicide.

Leaf stem rot, *crown rot*, *wilt* and *root rot* call for the rotten tissue and affected leaves and stems to be carefully removed, and the part concerned painted with a fungicidal solution or dusted with sulphur.

Pests and their control House plants are hosts to pests which may be imported with new plants or invade from outdoors. They can be controlled by using insecticides. Remove an infested plant from a room for treatment, either out of doors or in a well-ventilated cellar or shed, where the insecticide can be used without endangering the well-being of humans or pets, or despoiling household furnishings.

Ants Dusting the soil surface and base of plants with borax, or trichlorphon granules stops them.

Aphides (Greenfly) These insects suck the sap from young shoots and leaves, and sometimes act as the carriers of virus infections. Aphides may be controlled by spraying directly with an insecticide based on malathion, nicotine or derris. Alternatively, plants may be watered with a Systemic insecticide which introduces a trace of toxin into the sap stream for the aphides to imbibe.

Mealy Bugs These are sap-sucking insects which secrete a white, mealy wax covering and are found on the undersides of leaves and at the joints of stems in the summer months. Spraying with a malathion insecticide gives good control if repeated two to three times at intervals of ten to fourteen days.

Red Spider Mites These tiny, spider-like pests can infest house plants all the year around, sucking the sap to cause yellow spotting or speckling of the leaves. They may be controlled by contact application of a malathion or a derris insecticide, repeated at seven- to ten-day intervals two or three times or using a Systemic insecticide.

Slugs and Snails These molluscs are active at night, devouring foliage, tender shoots and bark. They succumb to metaldehyde or methiocarb bait pellets.

Tarsonemid Mites The cyclamen mite (*Tarsonemus pallidus*), milky white to brown in colour, and the broad mite (*T. latus*), of broader body and much faster movement, both cause leaves to become deformed, brittle, wrinkled or curled downward, and the flowers distorted. An insecticide based on Kelthane or a Systemic insecticide may be used.

Thrips Sometimes called Thunder Flies, these small, yellow, brownish or black, quick-moving, slender insects often appear in summer to attack a wide variety of plants, causing pale mottled, silver-white or bleached spots and areas on leaves, stunted shoots and distorted flowers. Spraying with a malathion or gamma-HCH (BHC) insecticide gives good control.

Vine Weevils The adult insects, dullish black, feed at night, eating small pieces out of the edges of leaves in spring. Then the females lay eggs in the soil, to hatch into small brown-headed, white grubs that feed from June onwards on plant roots until February. The adult insects can be controlled with a gamma-HCH (BHC) insecticide, the grubs by dressing the soil with a carbaryl or gamma-HCH (BHC) dust.

White Flies These small white flies, on the undersides of leaves, damage plants by sucking the sap. They are susceptible to gamma-HCH (BHC) malathion and dimethoate systemic insecticides.

Woodlice Otherwise known as slaters, monkey peas, sow-bugs etc., these crustaceans are easily controlled by dusting under and about pots with a gamma-HCH (BHC) insecticidal dust, so that they can pick it up on their feet as they move about.

Worms Although not directly harmful to plants, worms in a pot can be a nuisance. They can be flushed out by watering with a solution of potassium permanganate ($\frac{1}{4}$ oz per $\frac{1}{2}$ gal water), and picked off the surface as they are expelled.

Fungicides and insecticides are offered under proprietary names, with appropriate instructions which should be carefully followed.

Mimosa, Silver Wattle, Golden Wattle

Family LEGUMINOSAE

Acacia

Acacia armata

From this genus, those native to Australia can be easily grown in pots for house decoration. The flowers are small, yellow, but profuse and often fragrant, with attractive foliage in late winter and spring. Shrub-like and dwarf-growing are: *A. armata*, the Kangaroo Thorn, with a foliage of leaf-like expansions of the leaf-stalk, known as phyllodes, and rich yellow flowers from the axils; *A. longifolia*, the Sidney Golden Wattle, with long phyllodes and spikes of yellow flowers; and *A. pulchella*, with densely leaved spiny shoots, bearing round yellow flowers in axillary pairs. All call for a good compost (JIP No. 1), and should not be over-potted. They need sun, a winter temperature of 50° to 55°F (10° to 13°C) and moderate watering, increasing in spring. After flowering, plants should be pruned and thinned of loose, straggling growth, and in June placed out of doors, plunged in ashes, until late September. Propagate by seed, first soaked in warm water for four hours, in spring, or by cuttings of half-ripe shoots, taken with a 'heel' in July-August, in warm greenhouse.

Achimenes

Family GESNERIACEAE

Native to the tropical New World, *Achimenes* are herbaceous perennials with tuberous roots or stolons, of unusual flowering beauty, growing 12 to 24 in. tall, blooming freely in summer and autumn from February plantings. Mexican *A. longiflora* in its variety *major* is outstanding, with toothed, ovate leaves on stems of 12 to 15 in., and large, salver-shaped, violet-blue flowers; *A. erecta* of Jamaica, 18 in., bears geranium-red flowers of medium size freely; and *A. pedunculata* of Guatemala is tall, with orange-red and yellow flowers. The hybrid forms are richly beautiful and

Achimenes longiflora

varied. Plants may be started from tubercles planted 1 in. deep in JIP No. 1 compost, with growing tips to the centre in February, temperature of 55° to 60°F (13° to 15·5°C), grown in good light, with increasingly free watering and syringing of leaves on warm days. After flowering, plants die down and may be stored dry at 50°F (10°C) for winter. Propagate by seeds in early spring, or scales carefully rubbed off the tubercles and sown like seeds; by shoot cuttings in May-June, or leaves (with leaf-stalks inserted into the soil) in summer; temperature 65°F (18°C).

Myrtle Grass

Family ARACEAE

Acorus gramineus

Acorus gramineus

One of the two species of its genus—*Acorus calamus*, the Sweet Flag, is naturalized in Britain, the other —*A. gramineus*, the Myrtle Grass of Japan, is grown as a house plant in its variety *variegatus*. With its thin, grass-like leaves of about 8 in., striped cream and green, it is a useful plant to place in groups for foliage contrast. Being nearly hardy, it is suitable for the coolest indoor conditions, and, being a marsh or marginal water plant, can hardly be over-watered in growth. In its winter dormant period, however, much less water is needed though the soil must not be allowed to dry out. Propagate by the division of roots in March.

Maidenhair
Family POLYPODIACEAE

Adiantum

Of the 200 and more ferns that make up this genus, only a few species make easily managed house plants. With their thin, delicate fronds on numerous slender wiry stipes, the Maidenhairs are distinctive foliage plants for rooms receiving plenty of light but no direct sun, and are tolerant of temperatures ranging from 50°F to 75°F (10° to 24°C), kept moist. The hardiest is the North American *A. pedatum*, and potted plants may be brought in from a cold greenhouse

Adiantum capillus-veneris

in February to display their elegant pinnate fronds on slender polished stipes, 1 to 2 ft tall through summer and autumn. *A. capillus-veneris*, the native Maidenhair, and its forms, is accommodating but intolerant of low temperatures near freezing level. The Brazilian, *A. cuneatum* and its forms are deservedly popular, and are easily managed. Potted firmly but not hard in a mixture of equal parts by volume of loam, fibrous peat and sand, and re-potted annually in March; watered preferably by immersion, liberally in summer, moderately in winter; given airy, light conditions with no direct sun; and temperatures above 50°F (10°C), these ferns thrive and are decoratively pretty for indoors. Propagate by dividing roots with a sharp knife in March, or sowing spores.

39

Aechmea

Family BROMELIACEAE

Aechmea fulgens

Aechmea

These epiphytic ever-green plants of tropical South America are extremely handsome with their rosettes of sword-like leaves, and showy flowers which last long. They do best in moderate even temperatures above 45°F (7°C) and light shade. *A. fasciata*'s pale, silvery grey, lightly banded green rosette of foliage is a foil to its upright flower spike, clothed in rose-pink bracts with flowers of pink and blue from spring onwards. On *A. fulgens*, a native of Cayenne, the leaves are dark green, finely spined, and the flower a spike of flaming scarlet blooms throughout autumn. Naturally epiphytic, Aechmeas do best in organic composts, such as a mixture of equal parts by bulk sifted oak leaf mould, fibrous peat (or Osmunda fibre), half a part each sharp sand, and shredded sphagnum moss, and 4 oz. John Innes Base fertilizer per bushel. They like good light, moderate watering, with the central rosette kept full of water, and leaves free of dust. They are propagated by detaching the suckers produced around the base and potting in a mixture of equal parts by bulk of shredded sphagnum moss, oak leaf mould and fibrous peat, with bottom heat of 70° to 80°F (21° to 26·5°C).

Aeonium

Family CRASSULACEAE

Native to the Canary Islands, this genus contains a few species that make rosettes of fleshy leaves well adapted to use as window plants, and usually bear panicles of numerous flowers on leafy stalks in summer. One of the best is *A. undulatum*, which grows erect like a miniature tree with a flat rosette of dark green, smooth and shining fleshy leaves, 4 to 6 in. long, on a stem 2 to 3 ft tall, and a panicle of bright yellow tiny flowers on a leafy shoot of 12 to 18 in. in summer. *A. canariense* produces soft, flannelly,

Aeonium undulatum

fresh green leaves on short stubby stems, in rosettes growing to 3 ft across, and a panicle of pale yellow bell-shaped small flowers on an 18-in. leafy stem in spring; a useful plant for bold effect. Of branching, tufted growth, not more than 6 in. high, and 12 in. spread, with leaves in terminal rosettes, and golden flowers in short panicles in June, *A.* × *barbatum* is a tough, easily kept pot plant. These plants adapt themselves well to dry conditions, but are also happy in well-drained soil, at temperatures above 45°F (7°C), and like bright light, free watering in summer, but only little during the winter. Propagate by division, or leaves in spring.

41

Aloe

Family LILIACEAE

Aloe variegata

Aloe

This genus of evergreen succulent plants, native to South Africa or nearby islands, contains several species attractive for their fleshy leaves, usually arranged in rosettes, and welcome for their near hardiness and toughness under fluctuating indoor conditions. Of about 250 species some of the most suitable for house culture are *A. variegata*, the Partridge-breasted Aloe, with its dark green, stiff, keeled leaves, banded irregularly with white markings across; *A. humilis*, a dwarf, with very thick, blue-green leaves, beset with white teeth along the edges, and having varietal forms; and *A. mitriformis*, which grows upright with a stem, and has leaves spoon-shaped, green and edged with pale yellow teeth. The aloes like sun, free watering in summer, little in winter, and a temperature above 45°F (7°C). Propagate by the suckers in spring.

Belladonna Lily

Amaryllis

This genus is represented by the one species, *A. belladonna*, a bulbous plant native to South Africa, and esteemed for its beautiful, lily-like trumpet flowers borne at the head of strong, erect stalks in late summer. The strap-shaped leaves grow out after flowering, in autumn and winter. In the type, the flowers are rose-red and fragrant, but the species is variable and the white var. *blanda* is lovely, fading to blush pink, and *maxima* bears many flowers of a charming rose-pink; *pallida*, pale rose-pink; *rosea*,

Amaryllis belladonna

with flower segments striped white on rose and flowering in October; and *spectabilis* with flowers rose without and white within are all charming. For house culture, the bulbs are potted in large 8- to 10-in. pots in early summer while dormant, JIP No. 2 compost, and flowered in a cool, airy, well-lighted room, with liberal watering in pace with growth. After flowering, it should be kept growing until leaves die down, minimum temperature of 50°F (10°C). Re-potting is only necessary every third year. Water little during rest period. Propagate by offsets.

Flamingo Flower, Tail Flower

Family ARACEAE   *Anthurium*

Anthurium scherzerianum

Of the 500 species said to comprise this genus of tropical South American perennials, only one seems to be readily adaptable to house conditions—*A. scherzerianum*, native to Guatemala and Costa Rica. It has attractive long, leathery, oval and pointed, dark green leaves on wiry stems, and striking flowers, consisting of a brilliant scarlet open oval spathe with an orangy spadix rising above like a curly lamb's tail, on a tall stalk, which last long, and are apt to appear intermittently during the year. Many forms have been developed, offering different coloured flowers in rose, white and yellow. It is a plant that needs ample light, even temperatures with a winter minimum of a steady 60°F (15·5°C), and freedom from draughts. A rich porous compost, such as JIP No. 2, plus one fourth shredded sphagnum moss, is ideal, with provision for good drainage, and plants should be re-potted each spring in March. In summer, a moist atmosphere with syringing is beneficial; in winter, plants need to be kept mostly dry, with moderate watering. Propagation is easiest by division in January in a propagating frame in a warm greenhouse; though seeds sown with bottom heat of 80°F (26·5°C) give fine plants in time.

Aphelandra

Aphelandra

The most arresting of this genus of sixty evergreen tropical shrubs, offered as a house plant, is *A. squarrosa* var. *louisae,* which is Brazilian in origin. Strikingly exotic, it is of erect growth with large, lance-shaped, dark green leaves, having their central and lateral veins banded ivory-white, drooping in opposite pairs from the upright stem; while from the top pair arises a bright yellow bracted flower spike, $1\frac{1}{2}$ to 2 in. long, with yellow flowers opening from within the bracts over a period of two to

Aphelandra squarrosa

three weeks. After flowering, the spike should be cut out, just above the nearest pair of leaves, from the axils of which new shoots to flower next season will break. The plants are exacting in their needs, and need to be pot-bound to flower well. Ample light, but not direct sun, warm conditions with winter minimum of 55°F (13°C), and a good compost such as JIP No. 3, are suitable. Re-pot annually in spring, water increasingly with growth, and a weekly feed can be given when flower buds are in evidence. In winter, only moderate watering is needed. Propagate by heeled cuttings of young shoots in spring, with bottom heat 70°F (21°C).

Norfolk Island Pine

Family PINACEAE   *Araucaria*

Araucaria excelsa

Since the eighteenth century, the sub-tropical conifer, *A. excelsa*, commonly known as the Norfolk Island Pine which identifies its origin, has been a favourite room plant. Growing with a precise but beautiful symmetry, with horizontal branches, and drooping branchlets, densely lined with awl-shaped fresh green, short leaves, breaking from a central stem, young plants have an attractive ornamental elegance all the year round. Growing to 200 ft in its native habitat, a plant, even when curtailed by a pot, will grow rather tall in time. The variety *gracilis* is delightfully compact, *glauca* has blue-green foliage, and 'Silver Tips' is a form with the ends of shoots silvery white. A standard compost (JIP No. 2), a well-lighted, airy room, with moderate watering after re-potting, then free watering in summer, with a winter temperature of about 45°F (7°C), and occasional watering, are suitable for this amenable plant. Propagate by seeds sown in early spring (65°F (18°C), or by tip-cuttings, 6 in. long, taken from terminal shoots, in October.

Spear Flower

Ardisia

Family MYRSINACEAE

Containing about 240 species, this genus of evergreen trees and shrubs from tropical and sub-tropical regions gives us a fine decorative shrub for the house in *A. crispa* (syn. *A. crenulata*). Growing 2 to 3 ft tall in time, though rather slowly, it is furnished with tapering, lance-shaped, shining green leaves which are wavy-edged, bears fragrant reddish flowers in small terminal clusters in June, which then give way to small, bright red berries that persist the winter

Ardisia crispa

through; and with its compact habit, this Malayan and East Indies shrub is a favourite of those who know it. *A. japonica* of Japan is a dwarfer type, seldom growing more than 18 in. tall, with sharply toothed dark green leaves, white early summer flowers, and persistent red berries in autumn and winter. A soil compost as for rhododendrons (q.v.) suits best, with 5- or 6-in. pots, and plants need ample water and syringing in summer; but just keep moist in winter, with a minimum temperature of 50° to 55°F (10° to 13°C). Propagate by cuttings of side shoots in March, bottom heat 65°F (18°C), or seeds sown quarter of an inch deep.

Parlour Palm

Family LILIACEAE

Aspidistra

Aspidistra elatior var. *variegata*

Unperturbed by fumes or gas in the atmosphere, tolerant of light or deep shade, surviving much abuse or neglect in watering or temperatures, this genus of evergreen stemless herbs contains some of the most easily grown house plants. The species known to our Victorian forebears as the Parlour Palm, and to Americans as the Cast Iron Plant, is the Japanese *A. elatior*, with its tough, long, lanceolate sharp-pointed leaves arising in sheaves, and a well-grown plant may occasionally flower, though the flowers are inconspicuous, lurid purple bells produced in groups near the base of the leaves. Many people find the var. *variegata*, with alternate green and white striping on the leaves more interesting, but it must have good light and not be over-watered if the variegation is to be well retained. To give of its best, a plant should be potted in a standard compost (JIP No. 2), be watered freely in summer, only moderately in winter, and have its leaves wiped or sprayed free of dust as needed. Temperature minimum is about 50°F (10°C). Propagate by division in March.

Spleenwort

Asplenium

Family POLYPODIACEAE

Out of this genus of some 700 species of evergreen ferns, the most charming for indoors is probably *A. nidus*, the Bird's Nest Fern, from the Tropics of the Old World, striking for its flaring, bright green, undivided fronds, springing 2 to 4 ft long, creating a nest formation at the crown. It has a variety *australasicum* in which the midribs of the leaves are black. It requires

Asplenium nidus

moist, heated conditions, minimum winter temperature of 60°F (15·5°C), and shade, with liberal watering in summer, moderate in winter. Under similar conditions, the Australasian Spleenwort, *A. bulbiferum*, may be grown for its handsome pinnate leaves of 12 to 24 in. with their habit when mature of bearing little plantlets on their surface. For cooler frost-proof rooms, *A. trichomanes*, the Maidenhair Spleenwort, found in Britain, and its var. *cristatum* with crested fronds, are decorative small plants, and the Black Spleenwort, *A. adiantum-nigrum*, does well in pots. Propagate by division in March.

Bauera

Family SAXIFRAGACEAE

Bauera rubioides

Only two species make up this genus of small evergreen shrubs, native to New South Wales of Australia, and of these *B. rubioides* makes a handsome, small, 12- to 24 in. plant, with slender shoots, lined with three-partite opposite leaves, pointed and finely leaved, that appear whorl-like, and out of the axils of which grow white or pink, elfcap - shaped flowers singly, on wiry stalks, from late winter to early summer. Plants are best potted in October, JIP No. 2 compost, to be grown with partial shade for part of the day, winter temperature not more than 55°F (13°C); moderate watering, increasing in late spring and summer; and then place out of doors on warm, sheltered site until late September. Propagate by cuttings of ripening shoots in early autumn, bottom heat of 65°F (18°C).

Begonia, Bulbous and Winter-Flowering

Begonia Family BEGONIACEAE

The sole bulbous species is *B. socotrana*, from the Isle of Socotrana, which flowers at Christmas and into the New Year, with bright rose pink 2-in. flowers above dark green rounded leaves. It is a parent of winter-flowering hybrids; crossed with the South African *B. dregei*, it gave rise to × *B.* 'Gloire de Lorraine', characterized by reddish pink flowers freely produced, and varieties of it. Crosses with tuberous-rooted varieties resulted in such winter-flowering hybrids as 'Winter Gem', rose-scarlet.

Begonia 'Gloire de Lorraine'

All Begonias need fresh buoyant air, and a compost of two parts by volume medium loam, one part peat, one part leaf-mould, one part coarse sand, and 4 oz John Innes Base fertilizer per bushel. Winter-flowering Begonias potted in late summer need warm, airy but fairly humid conditions, minimum temperature 55°F (13°C), and roots kept nicely moist; after flowering the plants are rested until May, and stems cut back to 1 to 2 in. above the soil. As new growth is made plants need increased watering and shade from direct sun, with temperatures of 55° to 65°F (13° to 18°C). Propagate from shoot cuttings in summer, bottom heat 60°F (15·5°C); or leaf cuttings given bottom heat of of 70°F (21°C), in shaded propagating case.

Begonia, Tuberous

Family BEGONIACEAE

Begonia

Begonia davisii

The tuberous-rooted species deserving interest include *B. davisii* from Peru, with shining green leaves, red-flushed beneath, and bright, orange-red flowers and *B. froebelii* of Ecuador, with large scarlet flowers above broad, heart-shaped, bright-green and velvety leaves in winter; both are stemless. Other tuberous species have branching stems, such as *B. dregei* from South Africa, 2 ft tall, with small, toothed green leaves and cymes of small white flowers in summer; and the hybrid *B.* × *weltoniensis*, the Maple Leaf or Grape Leaf Begonia, with small light green leaves, and pink flowers in summer. *B. boliviensis* has drooping panicles of scarlet, fuchsia-like, from branching stems to 3 ft and *B. pearcei*, tall, bright yellow flowers on loose clusters in summer; both come from Bolivia. From the Far East, *B. evansiana* grows 2 ft with heart-shaped leaves, and many flesh-pink, large flowers in summer. Culture calls for good ventilation, temperatures between 50° and 65°F (10° to 18°C), partial shade, without over-watering and a rest period after flowers have finished. Propagate by leaf cuttings in summer; or by seeds.

Begonia, Rhizomatous Climbing or Trailing

Begonia   Family BEGONIACEAE

Begonias that grow with a creeping, swollen underground stem, or rhizome, from which they root and send up their flowering shoots, may be divided into those with long climbing or trailing stems, according to how they are grown, and those with erect-growing stems. Of the first, *B. glaucophylla*, a native of Brazil, is most commonly grown. From a short rhizome it sends out rather thin, long shoots, clothed in smooth, blue-green ovalish, deeply veined leaves, and many-flowered cymes of small coral or brick-red flowers from the leaf axils, in autumn or winter. It makes an interesting plant to droop naturally from a basket or high-placed container, or may be trained to grow up and along a window trellis, appreciating both warmth and sun. It requires a minimum winter temperature of 55°F (13°C), with watering regulated according to growth. Propagate by leaf cuttings in summer.

Begonia glaucophylla

Begonia, Rhizomatous Erect-Growing

Family BEGONIACEAE

Begonia

Begonia albo-coccinea

In this group we may consider the rhizomatous begonias which grow with erect stems and are pleasing in leaf and in flower. As house plants, the most suitable are *B. albo-coccinea*, of India, a low-growing plant with smooth, shield-shaped, 3- to 4-in. leaves, and four-petalled flowers, rose-pink without, white within, in dense clusters on 8-in. stems in summer; the Mexican *B. manicata* which is short-stemmed, with smooth, light green, fleshy, ovate, toothed leaves, and a tall flower stem that bears lacy cymes or sprays of small rosy-pink flowers in winter; *B. heracleifolia*, also of Mexico, has handsome radical, palmate, bronzy-green leaves on long hairy stalks, and panicles of small rosy-red flowers on a stem of 2 to 3 ft in summer; and a var. *nigricans* with leaves marked purplish-black, particularly near the margins. Given a well-drained compost, a minimum winter temperature of 50°F (10°C), a bouyant, humid atmosphere, with well regulated watering according to growth activity, and shade, these plants give good accounts of themselves in the home. Propagate by leaf cuttings in summer, for preference.

Begonia

Family BEGONIACEAE

Rhizomatous rooting plants are grown chiefly for their decorative foliage. Their flowers are unimportant, and are detached early to strengthen leaf growth. The most popular are *B. rex*, originally from Assam, and its many hybrids. Basically the leaves are radical, obliquely oval in shape, with heart-shaped base, coarsely toothed and tapering to a point, but it is in their magnificent colouring that attraction lies, banded, mottled, mar-

Begonia rex

gined in varied hues of green, pink to purple, silvery greys and often glistening metallically. Varieties are too numerous to list here, but typical are 'Silver Queen', silvery white and light maroon; 'Helene Teupel', dark green, silver and purple; 'Isolde', green and red with silver banding; and 'King Henry', dark green, banded silver and purple. Others are *B. daedalea*, Mexico, leaves green with a network of light maroon or russet brown, and *B. masoniana* (syn. *B.* × 'Iron Cross'), with roundish grey-green leaves having a dark-purple, medal-like cross-shaped zone. 55° to 60°F (13° to 15·5°C) suit these begonias best, and they need shade, with a buoyant humid atmosphere, maintained by careful watering, with plants stood on trays of pebbles, kept wet. Propagate by leaf cuttings.

Shrimp Plant

Family ACANTHACEAE   *Beloperone*

Beloperone guttata

This genus of about thirty tropical evergreen shrubs provides only one species, *Beloperone guttata*, introduced from Mexico in 1936, suitable for a house plant. It makes a small shrub of up to 2 ft high, with soft shining green oval leaves, and terminal arching spikes of flowers, 3 to 6 in. long, almost hidden by brownish-pink or salmon-coloured, overlapping bracts with some resemblance to a shrimp or prawn. It is easily grown, and starts flowering when quite young. Liking plenty of sun and light, it makes a good window-sill plant, with a winter temperature of 50°F (10°C). Pot and prune in spring, water increasingly with growth; occasionally in winter. Propagate by cuttings in spring and summer, bottom heat 65°F (18°C).

Billbergia

Family BROMELIACEAE

The most attractive plant for the house of this genus of over fifty species of stemless terrestrial tropical plants is *B. nutans*, a nearly hardy native of Brazil. It grows with rosettes of narrow, finely spined, grass-like, silvery-green leaves, about a foot long, and flowers in a drooping spike, made up of rose-pink bracts, surrounding small greenish yellow and blue flowers, in late winter and early spring. Its hybrid offspring, *B ×windii* (*B. decora ×B. nutans*) is broader-

Billbergia nutans

leafed, heavier and less erect in habit, but with a flower scape made up of bright rose-crimson bracts, greenish-yellow flowers, blue-tipped, 12 to 15 in. long, it is more showy, though not so graceful, nor quite so hardy. An organic compost (see *Aechmea*), potting and re-potting (every second year) in March, watering freely in summer, slightly less freely in winter, temperature 60°F (15·5°C) minimum. Propagate by offsets or suckers in spring, rooting with bottom heat 75°F (24°C).

Australian Native Rose

Family RUTACEAE

Boronia

Boronia elatior

A genus of Australian evergreen shrubs with four-petalled, open-faced flowers compared with a single rose. *B. elatior*, a branching shrub of up to 3 ft, with hairy shoots and small pinnate, linear-leafleted leaves, and rose-red to carmine small flowers in leafy spikes from the leaf axils in May; *B. megastigma*, a slender shrub of about 2 ft, with fine, narrow, blunt leaves and flower bells ½ in. wide, sweetly scented, flowers, chocolate brown without, yellow within, borne singly at the leaf axils; and *B. serrulata*, a bush of about 3 ft, with its stems densely clothed with small, almost stalkless, ovate leaves, and fragrant bright rose flowers, ½ in. wide, in terminal clusters of up to six, in June; make pleasant flowering plants for indoors, and may be stood out of doors after flowering until autumn. A peaty compost suits best, with good drainage. Pot in early spring, re-pot after flowering when necessary, and prune flowered shoots back. Water freely in active growth, more moderately in winter, with minimum winter temperature of 45° to 50°F (7° to 10°C). Well-lighted airy position preferred. Propagate by cuttings of firm, young shoots in summer, temperature 55°F (13°C), under shaded bell-glass or similar cover.

Bougainvillea

Family NYCTAGINACEAE

Bougainvillea

For an exotic effect indoors, the climbing species of this tropical genus of some eight species of shrubs are very useful. The easiest is *B. glabra*, which will flower when only 1 ft high, and continue to do as it grows, eventually to 6 to 10 ft; the inflorescence consists of comparatively insignificant tubular flowers, surrounded by showy rose-coloured bracts from June to August, against bright green foliage of rounded, oval leaves. In var.

Bougainvillea spectabilis

sunderiana flowering is especially free. *B. spectabilis* is even more showy, growing with greater vigour, and with very large panicles of lilac-rose bracted flowers in early summer, and dark green foliage. Potted in 7- or 8-in. pots, JIP No. 3, plants should be brought into warm rooms (60°F (15·5°C)), given as much light as possible and a light trellis or wire frame on which they may climb; water freely until September, then more moderately, with little in winter. Prune after flowering. After leaf-fall, plants may be kept in a room or cool greenhouse (temperature 50°F (10°C)), for the winter. Propagate by cuttings of half-ripened young shoots with a 'heel', in spring, bottom heat of 65°F (18°C).

Jasmine Plant

Family RUBIACEAE

Bouvardia

Bouvardia humboldtii
var. *corymbiflora*

Largely a Mexican genus of about thirty species the evergreen shrubs are commendable for their late autumn and winter flowering, and its freedom, in the warm greenhouse. Of them, *B. humboldtii* var. *corymbiflora* is a very fine form worth growing for the house, and with its fine ovate dark green, often whorled, foliage, and beautiful, tubular, jasmine-like, white flowers, nearly three inches long, in fragrant terminal racemes, on a branching plant of 2 to 3 ft high, it is very decorative during our shortening days of the waning year. *B. jasminiflora* has somewhat smaller flowers, but bears them very freely. Pot in March—April (JIP No. 2), to be grown on in a warm greenhouse or frame, with liberal watering, or in a well-sunned window (temperature 60° to 65°F (15.5 to 18°C)), for autumn flowering. Prune after flowering, water moderately, with temperature of 55°F (13°C) minimum. Propagate by cuttings of young shoots, 2 in. long, in spring, 70°F (21°C).

Bravoa

The only species of this small genus of Mexican bulbous plants in cultivation is *B. geminiflora*. It makes a graceful and somewhat unusual plant with linear, pointed, pale green leaves, and a flower stem adorned on the upper part with drooping, tubular, rich orange-red flowers in alternating pairs (from which it derives its common name of Twin-Flower) in July and August, growing 15 to 18 in. high. The plants are nearly hardy, and culture is simple. Pot three to four bulbs to a 6-in. pot in October, place in a cold frame or cold greenhouse, cover with ashes or coco-

Bravoa geminifolia

nut fibre, until January or February, then move to cool greenhouse or plant room (55° to 60°F (13° to 15·5°C)), water moderately, and flower in good light. Withhold water when leaves are yellow. Propagate by offsets when re-potting in autumn.

Caladium

Family ARACEAE

Caladium

Caladium × hybrida

From South America, the plants of this genus have tuberous roots, and handsome leaves. The chief species are *C. bicolor*, with green and red leaves, *C. picturatum*, green and yellow, and *C. schomburgkii*, green, white and silver, but they themselves have given rise to many varieties, and, as they cross-fertilize readily, to many hybrids to be chosen for the colouring and veining preferred. *C. humboldtii*, however, is a small, graceful type with light green leaves, with white centre and margins, useful for restricted settings such as a small table. The leaves are usually shaped like a shield or arrow-head and pointed, ranging in colour and variegations of green, cream, white, yellow, reds and purples. Plants become available from nurseries in early summer, and should be given full light in the home, with steadily increasing watering and syringing on hot days. They enjoy high temperatures (75°F (24°C)), and high humidity in growth. When leaves fade in autumn, water must be gradually withheld, and the dormant tubers stored in their pots, with a minimum temperature of 55°F (13°C), preferably in a warm greenhouse. They may be restarted into growth at 70°F (21°C), in JIP No. 3, with renewed watering. Propagate by dividing tuberous roots in spring.

Zebra Plant

Calathea

Family MARANTACEAE

Of this genus of South American herbs, distinctive for their beautifully coloured and textured leaves, one of the most striking is *C. zebrina* of Brazil, with long, lance-shaped leaves of deep emerald-green, striped with paler bands on the surface which are purple beneath, earning the plant the name of Zebra Plant. It is about 18 in. high. In

Calathea zebrina

C. ornata, of Colombia, the leaves are broadly ovate, very dark, almost purple, etched with fine pale pink lines between the veins, and deep purple underneath; it grows to 2 ft slowly, the leaves increasing in size. Several varieties are offered. *C. lindeniana*, with elliptical 6- to 8-in. leaves of deep green, marked much lighter zones, and purplish beneath, and *C. picturata*, with similar leaves but silvery-white line markings are elegant plants from Brazil. Exacting in their needs, they do best in a loose compost of equal parts by volume of peat, leaf-mould, medium loam and sand, with re-potting annually in spring; require humid and warm conditions in the home, well-lighted but out of direct sun, with minimum winter temperature of 60°F (15·5°C), out of all draughts. Watering should be free in summer, and the leaves washed regularly, but in winter, roots should be kept just moist. Propagate by division when re-potting.

63

Bell-Flower
Family CAMPANULACEAE

Campanula

Campanula isophylla

The genus runs to some 250 species, of which *C. isophylla*, a native of northern Italy, is a dainty, prostrate-growing, small-leaved perennial, happily adaptable to growing in the house, and exceedingly pretty when its trailing stems are covered with starry, salver-shaped, lilac-blue flowers all along their length in July and August. There is a white-flowering form, *alba*, and another, *mayi*, also white, but with variegated, soft woolly leaves. Pot in a standard well-drained compost (JIP No. 1) in March, grow under light airy conditions, watering freely in growth; after flowering, trim the shoots well back; give little water in winter, but keep frost-proof, temperature of at least 45°F (7°C), and re-pot in March-April for a new year of growth. Propagate by cuttings in spring, bottom heat of 60°F (15.°5C).

Chlorophytum, Spider Plant

Chlorophytum   Family LILIACEAE

Although some fifty species belong to this genus of tropical evergreen perennials, only one or two are in general cultivation. The plant considered the best for house decoration is correctly *C. comosum* var. *variegatum*, native to South Africa, and distinguished for its long, narrow linear leaves, smoothly green and striped white, and the curious flowering habit of producing separate stems at the ends of which grow small tufts

Chlorophytum comosum var. *variegatum*

of leaves which will root readily when placed on soil. This plant, however, is often offered under the name of *C. capense* var. *variegatum*, which is really the correct name for *C. elatum* var. *variegatum*, which again is often used as a synonym for *C. comosum*. The distinction can be made, however, from the fact that *C. capense* and its varieties have a leafless inflorescence, and only *C. comosum* and its forms bear the inflorescences with tufts of leaves. Plants are easily grown under light, airy conditions, and a minimum winter temperature of about 45°F (7°C). Watering is regulated by growth activity, increasing through spring and summer, with syringing on hot days, and decreasing with only very moderate watering in winter. Propagate by the tufted inflorescences, pegged on the soil in small pots, during summer.

Kangaroo Vine

Family VITACEAE

Cissus

Cissus antarctica

Of this genus of some 200 climbing plants, *C. antarctica*, the Kangaroo Vine of Australia, is deservedly popular, tolerating shade, a wide range of temperatures and even gas fumes in the atmosphere. As a branching climber with tendrils, it requires support, but leafs freely; the young leaves darken as they mature to a deeper leathery green, like a pointed beech leaf. *C. capensis* of South Africa is equally vigorous, but more of a trailer than a climber; its young kidney-shaped toothed leaves being pinkish-brown, turning bright green later, and the plant exhibits deciduous tendencies by losing its older leaves. Chile provides *C. striata*, which has small, five-fingered compound leaves of dark green on slender reddish stalks, freely produced on slender shoots, to be grown as a small climber or a bushy trailer. The hardier *Cissus* are happy with a winter minimum of about 45°F (7°C), and all prefer light but not direct sun; humid rather than dry conditions, with ample water in growth, though overwatering is disliked. In winter plants are kept much drier. Pot or re-pot in March-April, JIP No. 3 compost. Propagate by cuttings in spring, with young 2- to 3-in. shoots detached with a piece of the older branch, bottom heat of 65°F (18°C).

Orange, Lemon, Grapefruit

Citrus

Family RUTACEAE

The genus is one of evergreen shrubs or trees originating in sub-tropical and tropical regions of Asia. The Sweet Orange, *C. sinensis* makes a slow-growing shrub, or small tree, with dark green, ovalish pleasant foliage, and, when sufficiently mature, clusters of orange-blossom-scented, small white flowers which may give way to small, rather inedible fruits that turn gradually from dark green to orange-yellow. More recent-

Citrus sinensis

ly, another dwarf species has been offered under the name of *C. mitis*, which is said to remain dwarf and to flower and fruit readily. These plants are not difficult to grow under cool, airy, well-lighted room conditions, watered freely and syringed often when in active growth, with fortnightly feeding in summer; and then much more moderate watering and a temperature not falling below 50°F (10°C) in winter. Propagate by cuttings, when the plants are pruned to shape, in spring. The various edible forms of citrus—orange, lemon, grapefruit, tangerine—may be easily germinated from their pips, sown in pots of JIP No. 1 compost when available, with a temperature of about 65°F (15·5°C), and may be grown on as pleasant foliage plants.

Caffre Lily

Family AMARYLLIDACEAE

Clivia

Clivia miniata

Of the three species of this genus of South African bulbous plants with evergreen foliage, *C. miniata* and its varieties make pleasing and satisfactory house plants with their strap-like, deep green leaves, and spraying umbels of funnel-shaped and flared, yellow-throated, bright scarlet flowers, 2 in. or more long, twelve or more to an umbel, on scapes 12 to 18 in. high above the leaves, in late spring and summer.

There is a more golden-flowered form in var. *aurea*, and *C. × crytanthiflora* is a hybrid with more drooping flowers of salmon and flame. The somewhat rudimentary bulbs are potted in February, JIP No. 3 compost, and kept cool (55° to 60°F (13° to 15·5°C)), and allowed to become root-bound, with annual topdressing rather than re-potting. Watering should be liberal in the warm months, but plants kept more or less dry in winter with temperature of about 45°F (7°C). Propagate by division in February.

Croton, South Sea Laurel

Codiaeum
Family EUPHORBIACEAE

Only one species of this tropical genus of evergreen shrubs is generally in cultivation, and then as a variety—*C. variegatum* var. *pictum*. A native of Malaysia, it is esteemed for its fine foliage of entire, smooth leathery leaves which are variously marked in vivid colours, ranging through bright yellows, pinks, oranges, reds and crimsons in various combinations. The plant in cultiva-

Codiaeum variegatum var. pictum

tion has proved extremely variable, but some named forms are 'Earl of Derby', green, bright red and yellow mid-ribs; *carrierei*, orange, red and green; 'Triumphant Harwoodianum', green, with yellow network, suffused crimson; and 'Van Ostensee', thin linear leaves, green, spotted orange. Often sold by florists as Croton, plants are grown to a single stem, up to 2 ft high, and require ample light, high humidity, even temperatures with a minimum of 60°F (15·5°C) in winter, and complete freedom from draughts. They need much moisture by watering and syringing in summer; less in winter, though never being allowed to be dry. Propagate by cuttings of the young tops of shoots, dipping the ends in powdered charcoal, and inserting singly in small pots, JIP No. 1 compost, to root with bottom heat of 70°F (21°C), in moist propagating case.

Arabian Coffee Tree

Family RUBIACEAE

Coffea

Coffea arabica

There are up to forty species in this tropical genus of evergreen shrubs, but only one interests us here—*C. arabica*, the species developed as the source of the coffee beans or berries of commerce. Native to Abyssinia and Angola, it makes a highly attractive pot shrub, with opposite pairs of oblong, slender-pointed leaves, 3 to 6 in. long and half as much across, of dark glossy green, growing eventually to 5 ft tall or more. As it matures, small, white, pleasantly scented flowers appear close to the stem in September, and may be followed by red berries. It will grow quite well under airy, light conditions, out of direct sun, and cooler than its tropical origins would suggest, with summer temperatures of 65° to 75°F (18° to 23°C), and winter of 50° to 60°F (10° to 15·5°C), being kept well-watered in summer, and more moderately in winter, with little between November and March beyond keeping the soil just moist. Propagate by cuttings of firm shoots in summer in JIC compost with bottom heat of about 80°F (26·5°C), or by seeds in spring under similar temperture.

Cordyline

This genus of some dozen of evergreen shrubs, chiefly native to New Zealand and Australasia, is often confused with Dracaena, a related but largely African genus. The plants are handsome, with long assegai-shaped leaves, strongly channelled, and a palm-like habit of growth, the older leaves dying off a central stem from the base up. The most distinctive is *C. ter-minalis* which, under

Cordyline terminalis var.

house culture, grows 15 to 18 in. tall, with oval leaves having a tapered and curving tip, 12 in. or so long, 3 to 4 in. wide, plain green, but most beautifully coloured in its varieties, of which *baptistii* with deep green leaves striped pink and yellow, *norwoodiensis* striped in green and yellow with red margins, and *mayi* with young all-red leaves that become green in the centre as they age, are typical. *C. indivisa* of New Zealand is somewhat hardier with very long green and yellow leaves, and with *C. australis*, a compatriot with several colour-leaved forms, may be pot-grown for several years before becoming too tall and leggy. Pot in March in 6- to 10-in. pots, JIP No. 3, watering freely, and syringing foliage in the warm months, with partial shade; in winter 55° to 60°F (13° to 15·5°C) is needed, with moderate watering.

71

Crassula

Family CRASSULACEAE

Crassula lactea

Crassula

Of this large genus of succulent shrubs and herbs many may be grown indoors; the more attractive and easily managed are: *C. lactea*, of Natal, a shrub growing to 2 ft, with opposing fleshy, oval, abruptly pointed leaves of dark green with white dots, on thick stems, and terminal racemes of starry white flowers in winter; *C. falcata* of Cape Province has grey-green, sickle leaves and flat corymbs of scarlet flowers; and *C. arborescens*, also of the Cape, does not flower, but has decorative merit in its large, roundish, fleshy grey-green leaves, finely dotted and margined red, with stems stout to match. In contrast *C. cooperi* makes a low cushion of a plant with small, crowded pale green leaves and pale pink flowers in winter; *C. sarcocaulis* is a dwarf shrub with small pointed green leaves and white or pink flowers in summer; and *C. nealeana* is a pleasing prostrate trailer, white or pink flowering in summer. All hail from South Africa. Plants are potted in August-September, in a porous compost, and kept fairly dry in winter, minimum temperature of 45°F (7°C), increasing watering as new growth is made, but foliage must not be wetted, and over-watering strictly avoided. Propagate by division in spring or by cuttings of stem or leaf in summer.

Cryptanthus

Cryptanthus

Family BROMELIACEAE

Low-growing, stem-
less plants with
spreading rosettes of
leaves, often resemb-
ling the arms of a
starfish, and white or
greenish-white flow-
ers in the centre, the
species of this Brazil-
ian genus are all easily
grown house plants.
One of the most at-
tractive is *C. zonatus*,
with stiff leaves, finely
serrated, spreading 6

Cryptanthus bivittatus
var. *roseo-pictus*

to 9 in. long, with striated bands of green, white and
buff running across, and white flowers in summer; *C.
bivittatus*, with recurving leaves, has two broad stripes
to contrast with the green, running lengthways, and
has a var. *roseo-pictus*: *C. beuckeri* is a dwarf species,
with leaves more elliptical or shaped like a grapefruit
spoon, and beautifully marked; *C. tricolor* is larger with
leaves spreading to 10 in. long, striped lengthways with
dark green and cream, suffused pink at the centre and
margins; but *C. fosterianus* is the largest of all, with
leaves beautifully marked with horizontal irregular
bands of red and greyish white. Colouring varies in
intensity according to the exposure of the plants to
light, but none is difficult in a compost as for *Aechmea*
(q.v.), potting and re-potting in March, watering freely
in summer, and regularly at other times, with winter
temperature of 60°F (15·5°C), minimum. Propagate by
offsets in spring, bottom heat 75°F (24°C).

73

Comb-Flower

Family MARANTACEAE   *Ctenanthe*

Ctenanthe lubbersiana

This genus of Brazilian perennial herbs is closely related to that of *Calathea*, but differs in being of more tufted habit, with long - stalked basal leaves and short-stalked stem leaves. Its common name refers to the arrangement of the bracts of the flower, though this is of little significance, as the plants are grown chiefly for their foliage beauty. The pronunciation of the botanical name is made easier if the 'c' is treated as more or less silent. The species usually cultivated include *C. lubbersiana*, growing overall to 15 to 18 in. high, with stalked, linear-ovate bladed leaves, up to 8 in. long and 3 in. across, with a pale green ground colour, a foliage specimen of tapering shape for cool rooms and halls. It likes light, airy surroundings, and needs only a minimum temperature of 45° to 50°F (7° to 10°C) in winter. Propagated by seeds sown in spring, bottom heat 65°F (18°C), or by cuttings of young shoots taken in August.

74

Cigar Plant

Cuphea

Family LYTHRACEAE

Of this mixed genus of some ninety annual and perennial herbs and evergreen shrubs, only a few are grown for house decoration. The most popular is *C. ignea*, a somewhat slight shrubby evergreen of 12 in. high, with small lanceolate leaves, and alight for several weeks in summer with bright scarlet, bluish-black and white tubular flowers that inspire its common name of Cigar plant; it has also a white-flowering var. *alba*. *C. micropetala* is of similar free and

Cuphea ignea

graceful branching habit, with flowers of scarlet, yellow and white, and *C. miniata* grows up to 2 ft, with pale vermilion flowers from the leaf axils. None of these Mexican plants is difficult, potted in March-April, in JIP No. 2 compost, and given good light, and ample watering in the warm weather months; in winter only moderate watering, with a minimum temperature of 50°F (10°C), is needed. Propagate by cuttings of young heeled shoots in August or April, bottom heat of 65°F (18°C), or by seeds sown in March under glass.

Mourning Cypress, Chinese Weeping Cypress

Family PINACEAE *Cupressus*

Cupressus funebris

Member of a genus of about twelve species of evergreen conifers, *C. funebris*, the Mourning Cypress of Central China, is a gracefully growing plant with fine grey-green foliage, too tender for outdoors, but making a most charming juvenile specimen when grown in pots. As a forest tree, it will eventually grow too tall for the house, but it takes several years about it, and meanwhile flourishes as a beautiful foliage specimen of tapering shape for cool rooms and halls. It likes light, airy surroundings, and needs only a minimum temperature of 45° to 50°F (7° to 10°C) in winter. Propagated by seeds sown in spring, bottom heat 65°F (18°C), or by cuttings of young shoots taken in August.

Cyclamen

Of this genus of tuberous rooted deciduous plants, the most suitable for house display is *C. persicum* in its highly developed and selected varieties. The type itself, native to eastern Mediterranean countries, is notable for its large, winged flowers with reflexed petals, borne on 6- to 8-in. stems in a succession that lasts for several weeks through winter and spring, above heart-shaped, darkish-green foliage; several named varieties have been bred. Growing plants are brought into

Cyclamen persicum

the home in flower in autumn or early winter, when they are best in partial shade, with good ventilation but no draughts, regular watering without wetting the crowns, and a temperature of 50° to 55°F (10° to 13° C). Plants should be placed in a cold frame in May or out of doors in June, and when growth yellows, water is withheld. In August, tubers may be re-potted, JIP No. 3 compost, firmly, with the surface level with the soil surface; soak and grow on with increasing watering, in shade with temperature of not more than 55°F (13°C), until flower buds show it is ready for the house. Propagate by seeds, sown in August-September in shade, under glass, temperature 55°F (13°C), need to be grown without faltering.

Holly Fern: Wood Fern

Family POLYPODIACEAE

Cyrtomium

Cyrtomium falcatum

Regarded by some authorities as a genus of ten species and by others as one of one species with nine varieties, the representative usually listed is *C. falcatum*, a fern found in Japan and countries including India, China, Celebes and Hawaii, with handsome evergreen fronds, 12 to 24 in. long, 6 to 8 in. broad, and pinnate with sickel-shaped glossy pinnae. It is excellent for the house, and will even grow quite well in unheated rooms, and in shade. Varieties—or species, according to which authority you follow—include *caryotideum* which has fronds that are drooping in habit, with rather larger pinnae, *fortunei* with narower and dull green pinnae, and *pendula* with distinctly hanging fronds. None is difficult requiring only light shade, a simple compost of equal parts by volume loam, peat and sharp sand, and moderate watering, with rather more in the warmer months of active growth; the soil is just kept moist in winter, with a temperature minimum of 45°F (7°C). Propagate by spores in spring.

'Genista'

Cytisus

Family LEGUMINOSAE

Cytisus canariensis

Together with the genera *Genista* and *Spartium*, this genus is collectively known as Broom. To confuse maters, however, florists give the name 'Genista' to one of its species, *C. canariensis*, a lovely, free-branching, half-hardy, evergreen shrub, from the Canary Isles, of 3 to 6 ft, which may be grown to flower and grace well-lighted rooms indoors. Its pea-like flowers are borne in short racemes of bright yellow on young shoots in March to May, against tri-foliolate leaves. Its hybrid form, *C.* × *racemosus* (*C. canariensis* × *C. maderensis magnifoliosus*), is similar but with looser racemes of flowers. Young plants are potted in spring, and may spend the summer out of doors, plunged in ashes, to be brought in for flowering in September, placed in a shaded room, watered moderately, temperature 50°F (10°C); in January they are moved to good light, and greater warmth (55° to 60°F (13° to 15.5°C)), and watered increasingly as new growth is made. After flowering, flowered growth is cut back to within a bud or two of its base, and plants may be re-potted in JIP No. 1 compost. Other brooms, such as the Teneriffe Broom, can be grown in pots similarly. Propagate by seeds in spring or summer; cuttings in August.

Hare's-Foot Fern

Family POLYPODIACEAE

Davallia

Davallia canariensis

One of a genus of thirty-six ferns, chiefly native to the tropics of the Old World, *D. canariensis*, popularly the Hare's-Foot Fern, alluding to the rhizomatous roots which climb over the sides of a pot and are covered with fine, silky brown hair, is pleasing with its ornamental green fronds, of 12 to 18 in., and makes an excellent room plant. Potted in March, in JIP No. 1, or a compost of equal parts by volume peat, leaf-mould, and sandy loam, plus a little charcoal, it is happy in partial shade and cool conditions, with liberal watering in summer, moderating in winter when the temperature should not fall below 50°F (10°C). Propagate by division of the roots in March-April, or by spores in a propagating case in spring or summer.

Dumb Cane

Dieffenbachia Family ARACEAE

This genus of erect-growing, evergreen perennials of the Arum family is native to tropical America, and contains some effective foliage plants for the house where a minimum temperature of 55°F (13°C) can be consistently maintained. They have become known as Dumb Plants or Dumb Canes—Numbing would be a better term—from the fact that the sap is poisonous, and any part of a plant, bitten or sucked, causes intense

Dieffenbachia picta

pain and swelling, with loss of desire to talk. *D. picta*, Brazil, is the best-known, with dark green, long, slender-pointed leaves, much spotted with pale green, white or cream markings, on a fleshy stem, and has several varieties. *D. seguine*, the true Dumb Cane, is best in its vars. *barraquiniana*, with bright lightish green spotted white leaves, and *liturata*, with satiny green leaves striped white. Pot in March, JIP No. 3 compost, grow in partial shade, with humidity, frequent watering in active growth and with high temperatures, with syringing of foliage; more moderate watering in winter. Propagate by cuttings, or top portions of over-tall stems, or by suckers from the base of plants, inserted in JIS compost, bottom heat of 85°F (29°C).

Threadleaf

Family ARALIACEAE *Dizygotheca*

Dizygotheca elegantissima

The precise number of species of this genus of shrubs, native to the islands of the South Seas, seems uncertain, between three and eleven, and formerly listed under Aralia. The most outstanding as a house plant is *D. elegantissima*, slow-growing with an erect, slender stem carrying compound digitate leaves on long, dark green, mottled white, thready stalks, split into seven to ten slender, toothed arching leaflets which become broader as they age. *D. kerchoveana* is also graceful with its leaflets of glossy green wavy-edged and serrate; and *D. veitchii* is most charming with its leaflets shining green and dark red beneath, and has a particularly fine-leafleted form in var. *gracillima*, but plants are not readily available. These shrubs are somewhat exacting, requiring moist, warm atmosphere, good light, liberal watering, though rather less in winter than in summer, and a winter minimum temperature of 55°F (13°C). Propagate by cuttings in closed propagating case, temperature 75°F (23°C), in JIC compost.

Dragon Plant

Dracaena

Family LILIACEAE

In nature these plants are tree- or shrub-like. As house plants, they are grown for their fine foliage. From Guinea we have *D. fragrans*, usually offered in its vars. *lindenii*, with recurving dark green leaves, having a yellow central striping along the mid-rib; and *massangeana*, with somewhat broader leaves, striped whitish down the centre. The Congo furnishes *D. godseffiana*, a low, slender spreading plant with oval, 3- to 4-in.-long leaves of dark green, thickly spotted bright cream, and *D. sanderiana*, a smaller, slender plant with leaves 6 to 9 in. long but only $\frac{1}{2}$ to $1\frac{1}{2}$ in. wide, green with a broad white margin. *D. goldieana* is a pleasing slender plant with broad, long ovate leaves of glossy green, banded across with silver-green, and a mid-rib of yellow, from West Africa, and the same region provides *D. deremensis* which grows most attractively. Potted in March, JIP No. 3 compost, they enjoy semi-shade, a humid atmosphere and warmth, with leaves sponged often, and a winter minimum of 50° to 55°F (10° to 13°C), though revelling in higher temperatures where available. Propagate by cuttings of the tops taken off old plants in April, inserted in JIC compost, bottom heat 75°F (23°C).

Dracaena deremensis

83

Dryopteris: Buckler Fern

Family POLYPODIACEAE

Dryopteris

Dryopteris sieboldii

This tremendous genus of world-wide distribution runs to over 1200 species, but only a few need be considered as house plants, for the decorative effect of their leaves or fronds. *D. sieboldii*, native to Japan and China, makes a good evergreen, with fronds up to 12 in. long and 2 in. broad; and its compatriot, *D. erythrosora*, is very decorative, as its fronds change from bronzy-green when young to dark green as they age. The native Buckler Fern, *D. spinulosa*, is graceful with divided fronds, and has several varieties. Although sub-tropical, *D. parasitica* is easily grown and in its var. *corymbifera*, the apices of the fronds and pinnae are delightfully crested. Two Australasian species *D. decomposita* and *D. glabella*, make easily grown, decorative pot ferns with neat habit and finely cut fronds. Potting calls for a compost of equal parts by volume of loam and peat, and half a part of sharp sand, three ounces bonemeal to the bushel, and a little charcoal. The ferns are indifferent to shade, but need buoyant air and regular watering, less in winter, but no spraying and a winter temperature not less than 50°F (10°C). Propagate by division in spring, or by spores.

84

Dyckia

Family BROMELIACEAE

Native to South America, the some eighty species of this genus of stemless, succulent perennials are characterized by rather elegant, thick, spiny leaves, growing in a rosette from a rhizomatous root, and with orange or yellow flowers in summer. The species most acceptable as house plants are *D. remontiflora* (syn. *D. rariflora*) of the Argentine and Uruguay with a rosette of sharply spined narrow leaves, 6 to 9 in. long, recurving gracefully, and deep orange, bell - shaped flowers on a loose spike of 18 to 24 in. high; and

Dyckia brevifolia

D. sulphurea of like origin, which has a many, densely leaved rosette with grey-green, narrow leaves of 8 to 10 in., and pale yellow flowers in a loose raceme on a stalk of 12 in. or so. These plants grow quite happily, potted in March, JIP No. 2, in good light airy rooms, with liberal watering in active growth, but little in winter, when the temperature should not fall below 50°F (10°C). Propagate by offsets or suckers in spring.

Echeveria

Family CRASSULACEAE

Echeveria retusa

This genus of succulents, of south and west North America, provides several house plants attractive for their rosettes of fleshy, coloured leaves and gaudy flowers. *E. retusa hybrida* of unknown parentage has large spatulate, blue-green, red-margined leaves, and bell-shaped, crimson flowers, 2 ft high, in winter. *E. setosa* is remarkable for its rosette of white-bristle covered leaves and showy re-tipped yellow flowers in summer. *E. gibbiflora* var. *carunculata* is shrubby with curious blister-like markings on its waxy leaves; and *E. elegans* is a stemmed plant 1 ft tall with concave white and green leaves, and pink, yellow-tipped, summer flowers. *E. agavoides* with a close low rosette of triangular, pale-green, brown and sharp-pointed tipped leaves, with reddish-yellow flowers, and *E. carnicolor* with a low cluster of rosettes of fleshy, pink waxy leaves and orange-red March flowers, are excellent for small pots. Grown in JIP No. 2 compost, in good light, with airy coolness, and watered from beneath to avoid wetting the leaves, these plants are little trouble, though the temperature must not go below 50°F (10°C). Propagate by leaf or stem cuttings, or offsets where produced, in spring or summer.

Hedgehog Cactus: Barrel Cactus

Echinocactus Family CACTACEAE

Reclassifications among the Cactus family have left this genus one of about nine species native to Mexico, Texas and California. They make large, round or cylindrical ribbed plants, with very spiny areoles and densely woolly crowns, and are interesting as pot plants. *E. horizonthalonius* of Mexico and Texas has about eight rounded ribs, a somewhat squat or globu-

Echinocactus horizonthalonius

lar formation, and stout, curved spines of which the central one of each cluster is stouter and longer; the flowers from the top are pale pink on a mature plant in summer. *E. grusonii* is many ribbed, with globose shape, and golden yellow spines, eventually growing quite large, when it may produce its yellowish flowers. *E. grandis* of California may grow to quite a large specimen, about 3 ft, in time, and changes somewhat from a dull green, horizontally banded barrel when young to a thinly-ribbed structure, with stout spines with woolly bases, and yellow flowers in summer. A porous compost, with re-potting every third year, a sunny warm position, about weekly watering in summer and monthly in winter, with a minimum temperature of 50°F (10°C), suit these plants. Propagate by seeds in spring or summer.

Echinocereus

Family CACTACEAE

Echinocereus

Echinocereus pectinatus

Consisting mainly of low-growing plants, with rounded and ribbed stems, this genus of about thirty species of cacti native to Mexico and Texas provides a few worth growing in the house on sunny warm window-sills. *E. pectinatus* is one of the most beautiful and free-flowering, with a many-ribbed, columnar stem and clusters of white or pink spines in bands round the plant, the large pink flowers appearing in summer. *E. rigidissimus* is similar in growth, but the colouring of its spines in alternate rows of pale pink and brownish-red earn it the name of 'Rainbow Cactus'. Other easy species are *E. reichenbachii* with stiffly erect stem, with white or brown spines and fragrant light purple flowers, *E. blanckii* with stems tending to sprawl and branch freely, and violet-purple flowers 2 to 3 in. across from the older stems, and *E. pentalophus* growing procumbent with few ribbed, short stems and reddish-violet flowers produced readily. Cultivation calls for full sun when in active growth and regular weekly watering; in winter the plants are kept much drier, with occasional watering once every four to six weeks, with a minimum temperature of 50°F (10°C). Propagate by seeds or cuttings.

Australian Heath

Epacris

Family EPACRIDACEAE

These evergreen shrubs originating in Australia, Tasmania or New Zealand make charming winter-flowering pot plants for the home. Typical types are *E. impressa* upright-growing with branching stems, lined with small, spear-shaped, sharply pointed, alternating leaves and bearing beautifully moulded, tubular flowers ½ in. long, white to red, singly from the leaf axils, *E. longiflora* taller-growing with rosy-crimson flowers, and *E. purpurascens* with closely set leaves and white, flushed red flowers. There are many beautiful garden forms and the plants make most attractive columnar bushes of colour for December to March.

Epacris impressa

Flowering plants may be bought in early winter and grown under cool, airy and light conditions, temperature about 50°F (10°C), with moderate watering only; after flowering, shoots are pruned to within an inch of their base; re-potting (biennially) April-May, in lime-free compost, and plants may be placed in a cold frame or plunged out of doors from late June to September, when they are brought in again. Summer temperatures of about 60°F (15·5°C). Propagate by cuttings of the ends of shoots in spring inserted in JIC compost, bottom heat of 55°F (13°C), or by seeds sown in a compost of equal parts by volume fine peat and sand.

Leaf-Flowering Cactus: Orchid Cactus

Family CACTACEAE   *Epiphyllum*

× *Epiphyllum ackermannii*

This genus is native to tropical America and usually epiphytic. Of the species, *E. oxypetalum* with flat, thin, broad stems, branches freely and bears large white flowers that open and scent the air in the evening; and *E. crenatum* with deeply indented, broad, flat stems bears large, cream to yellow, fragrant flowers. But the finest Epiphyllums stem from × *E. ackermannii*, a hybrid of an *Epiphyllum* sp. × *Heliocereus speciosus*, producing very large crimsonred flowers on typical flattish, crenated stems. In turn, this plant is a parent of many cultivated hybrids, such as 'Cooperi', white; 'Adonis', pink; 'Flamingo', scarlet; *peacockii*, carmine and violet; 'Oriole', yellow, gold and white; 'Northern Lights', rose and lavender; and 'Valencia', orange to red. A compost of two parts each by volume of loam, leaf-mould and coarse sand, and one part each of broken charcoal and crushed brick-rubble, suits well. Liberal watering and frequent spraying during growth in summer, in semi-shade; in winter, very little or no water should be given, minimum temperature 45° to 50°F (7° to 10°C). Propagate by cuttings of mature stems in early spring with bottom heat of 60°F (15·5°C).

Cape Heath

Erica

Family ERICACEAE

Native to South Africa, the winter-flowering Cape Heaths, suitable for warm greenhouse or home, have been extensively grown. *E. gracilis* makes a bushy shrub of 12 to 18 in. with tiny leaves in fours along its erect stems and terminal flower clusters of egg-shaped, deep pink bells on small side shoots, October to December; var. *nivalis* bears white flowers. *E. hymenalis* has upright stems carrying tapering racemes of tubular, white, rose-tinted, drooping flowers in November to February, and a rose-pink form in *rosea*. For later flowering there

Erica hymenalis var. *rosea*

is the hybrid *E. × cavendishiana* which bears rich yellow flowers; *E. massonii* with reddish, white and green flowers in umbels; and *E. ventricosa* blooming from June onwards in varieties with white, pink, rose-red and rose-purple colours. All these heaths welcome light, airy but cool conditions, a winter temperature of 45° to 50°F (7° to 10°C) and a summer of 55° to 60°F (13° to 15·5°C), but must not be allowed to become dry. Watering is done by plunging pots into water and draining, frequently. After flowering, shoots should be pruned to within 1 in. of their base, and plants repotted in a lime-free compost. Propagate by shoot cuttings 1 to 2 in. long in spring, bottom heat of 60°F (15·5°C).

Coral Tree

Family LEGUMINOSAE

Erythrina

Erythrina cristagalli

The chief plant of this genus of thirty tropical species of the Pea family grown as a house plant is *E. cristagalli*, the Coral Tree of Brazil, which as a pot plant may grow gradually to 4 or 5 ft tall. The leaves are trifoliolate with leathery, bluey-green leaflets and the plant blazes with large, beautiful racemes of brilliant deep scarlet, pea-like flowers through early summer. Potted in March in a standard compost, JIP No. 1, the plant may be started into renewed growth in temperature of 55° to 60°F (13° to 15·5°C) under light, airy conditions with increasingly liberal watering. After flowering, it may be stood out of doors in a sheltered, sunny place until September when it should be wintered while leafless under frost-proof conditions (45° to 50°F (7° to 10°C)) and kept almost dry. Flowered shoots die back each year and should be cut away in autumn. Propagate by cuttings of young shoots with a heel in spring, with bottom heat of 70°F (21°C), or by seeds.

Scented Gum

Eucalyptus
Family MYRTACEAE

Eucalypti, or Gum Trees, comprise a genus of over 500 species, mostly tall evergreen trees, but in it is found *E. citriodora*, a charming native of Queensland, which may be grown in small pots as a shrub, chiefly for the sake of its strongly but pleasantly lemon-scented foliage, the leaves being more or less lance - shaped growing opposite in the juvenile state and alternate in the adult. Another species, *E.*

Eucalyptus citriodora

globulus, the Blue Gum, with young shoots and leaves a bluish-white, is grown for its foliage beauty as a young plant. Young plants may be bought in pots, but are readily raised from seeds grown $\frac{1}{8}$ in. deep, in JIS compost, in spring or August, temperature 65°F (18°C). Plants thrive in light, airy rooms, with winter temperatures of 45° to 50°F (7° to 10°C), with moderate watering only, but more liberal watering from April onwards. As a rule no pruning is necessary.

Amazon Lily

Family AMARYLLIDACEAE *Eucharis*

Eucharis grandiflora

All species of this genus of bulbous plants are worth growing for their beauty and fragrance. Natives of Columbia they flower in winter and spring. The species most commonly available are: *E. grandiflora*, with broadly ovate, slender-pointed and channelled leaves on long stalks, and large, white, narcissus-like, drooping flowers in umbels of four or six at the head of scapes 2 ft tall. By potting bulbs at different times, the flowering can be spread over several months. Smaller-leaved and smaller-flowered varieties are listed under *lowii* and *moorei*. *E. candida*, with a solitary long-stalked leaf, has more but smaller white flowers; and *E. sanderi* grows like *E. grandiflora*, but with three to seven smaller yellow-white flowers on 18-in. scapes. Three to six bulbs may be potted to a 6-in. pot, in JIP No. 3 compost, and left undisturbed until completely root-bound, before potting to a bigger pot, preferably in spring. Growth is started in a temperature of 70°F (21°C), and watering gradually increased with growth. The plants like warm, humid conditions with spraying of foliage in summer, and being evergreen require only a short rest, with a temperature in winter of 55° to 60°F (13° to 15·5°C). Propagate by offsets when re-potting.

Euphorbia

Euphorbia

Family EUPHORBIACEAE

Over 1000 species are assigned to the genus which includes annual and perennial herbs, shrubs and trees, non-succulent and succulent. Of the succulent kinds *E. meloformis* of Cape Province grows with a globular, ribbed main-stem, and is glossy-green with transverse bands of lighter green and purple, but the flowers

Euphorbia meloformis

produced on long stalks are small and the stalks later become spine-like. *E. obesa* is similarly globular but the ribs are much less prominent, and *E. globosa* is a dwarf that branches with oval stems, ribbed along their length. *E. mammillaris* with rounded stems tubercled like cobs of sweet corn becomes well spined with the persistent stalks of spent flowers. Some species are of prostrate or trailing habit, and of these *E. caput-medusae* makes a pretty plant with radially disposed, spiny grey-green branches and small whitish flowers in summer. These plants are easily grown in JIP No. 1 compost under cool, airy conditions, and do not need too much water, with very little in winter when a minimum temperature of 50°F (10°C) suffices. Propagation needs to be studied, for while several increase from cuttings, dried off for a few days before insertion in JIS compost, others need to be grown from seeds.

Euphorbia (Shrub Type)

Family EUPHORBIACEAE

Euphorbia splendens

Of the shrubby types of Euphorbia, *E. splendens* of Madagascar is known as 'Crown of Thorns' from its brown, branching, succulent stems with long spines. A few small green leaves appear to the tips of branches, and small flowers, each enclosed in a pair of blood-red bracts, are borne in branching clusters December to June. *E. fulgens*, the Scarlet Plume of Mexico, is a charming shrub with lance-shaped leaves and bright scarlet-bracted flowers in clusters in winter. There is also the Poinsettia, *E. pulcherrima*, a deciduous shrub notable for its showy bright scarlet bracts that surround the small yellow flowers in autumn and winter; there are double varieties. The enemies of these plants are draughts and widely fluctuating temperatures. In winter and while in flower, moderate watering and a temperature range of 55° to 60°F (13° to 15.5°C) suits well; when flowers and bracts fade less water should be given and flowered shoots on *E. fulgens* and *E. pulcherrima* may be pruned. Then after resting, and with new growth, watering becomes liberal and increasing with temperature rises. Propagate by cuttings of young shoots, taken with a 'heel', after drying off a few days, in spring; bottom heat of 65°F (18°C).

*× **Fatshedera**

Family ARALIACEAE

Fatshedera

The sole member of this genus is × *F. lizei*, an unusual bigeneric hybrid originating from a crossing of *Fatsia japonica* var. *moseri* with *Hedera hibernica*, made at the nursery of Messieurs Lizé Frères, Nantes, France about 1910, and recognized in the plant's epithet. It is quite hardy and makes an evergreen shrub of somewhat loose growth with dark, lustrous green, palmate leaves with five lobes on long stalks and somewhat thin stems that need some support as they

× *Fatshedera lizei*

lengthen. In favourable conditions it may put out round umbels of green flowers about 1 in. wide, that together make large terminal panicles of bloom in October and November. It is a useful plant grown in a large pot for cool rooms and shade, needing a minimum winter temperature of 45°F (7°C) and very moderate watering until growing anew in April. During the summer it can be stood out of doors until September, in semi-shade, wind-sheltered. Propagate by cuttings of shoots, severed just below leaf nodes, in spring and summer.

* × indicates that the plant is a hybrid in botanical nomenclature.

Fig-Leaf Palm: Japanese Aralia

Family ARALIACEAE   *Fatsia*

Fatsia japonica

Of the two species in this genus, one is *F. japonica*, an evergreen, almost hardy shrub of Japan that makes a splendid foliage plant for the house particularly as it tolerates shade. With stout stems and large, shining leathery leaves of deep green, palmately and deeply cut with seven or nine lobes, it grows well in pots, and is excellent for cool rooms and hallways with a winter temperature of not less than 45°F (7°C). Plants may be potted in March, April, JIP No. 3 compost and re-potted as the roots fill the smaller container. Older plants with spreading habit and matured wood may bear their round umbels of white flowers in October and November. Var. *moseri* is of more compact habit but with even larger leaves, and there is a coloured form, *variegata*, with the leaves pleasantly marked by cream margins. Propagate by cuttings of shoots severed below leaf nodes in spring and summer, or by seeds, bottom heat 65°F (18°C).

Barrel Cactus

Ferocactus

Family CACTACEAE

American authorities place thirty species of their Barrel Cacti in this genus, which are natives of southern states such as Mexico, Texas, Arizona and California, distinguished by their round or cylindrical columnar shape, tending to grow large, with thick, prominent ribs strongly spined often hooked. The flowers are also large,

Ferocactus melocactiformis

bell-shaped and appear at the top of mature plants, but as these may be some feet high the flowers are seldom seen in cultivation. A useful selection for pot growth in the home is: *F. acanthoides*, many-ribbed stem, with large areoles with dense brown wool and spines of pink or red, that may grow inches long; *F. latispinus*, with rounded stem, prominently ribbed, with radial spines of six to ten, white to pink, and a central spine that is either flattened or hooked; *F. melocactiformis*, with pleasing blue-green cylindrical stem, up to twenty-four ribs, and spines that are yellow, turning brown with age; and *F. wislizenii*, a globular form, with many ribs, and spines vari-coloured, white to red. None is difficult given light, airy quarters, a porous compost, moderate watering in summer, and little in winter; minimum temperature 45°F (7°C). Propagate by seeds, by cuttings.

Fig, Indiarubber Plant

Family MORACEAE *Ficus*

Ficus elastica var. *decoria*

The figs comprise over 600 species, distributed in sub-tropical and tropical regions. Several make excellent house plants. The easiest to grow is *F. elastica* var. *decora*, the Indiarubber plant of tropical Asia, with a thick woody stem from which arise spirally stiff, leathery, oblong, pointed, dark shiny green leaves with touches of red when unfolding and young. A plant may grow 8 to 12 ft for it is a forest tree in nature; there are variegated forms, notably var. *doescheri*, with leaves of green and a creamy margin, needing rather more care. *F. lyrata*, the Fiddleleaf or Banjo Fig, of western tropical Africa is distinctive for its very large, stiff, fiddle-shaped leaves of glossy green with conspicuous whitish veins, up to 2 ft long, on a single erect stem, but grows slowly. Potted, and re-potted, in March-April, JIP No. 3 compost, all these figs grow well in light, airy conditions free of draughts and a temperature range of 50° to 70°F (10° to 21°C). A policy of moderate watering with frequent spraying of the leaves in spring and summer, and occasional waterings letting the soil almost dry out in between in winter, is successful. Propagate by top stem or shoot cuttings inserted in JIC compost in spring, with bottom heat of 80°F (26·5°C).

Climbing Fig

Ficus

Family MORACEAE

Here may be grouped the Figs that grow chiefly by slender, drooping or climbing stems. The species generally grown is *F. pumila*, native to China and Japan, and totally dissimilar from the tree species with its thin stems, small, heart-shaped leaves about an inch long, and fine branches that creep or, being equipped with aerial roots like Ivy, can cling and climb. Relatively hardy and welcoming shade it is one of

Ficus pumila

the best climbing plants for the house. Another creeper —or climber—is *F. radicans* from the East Indies with 2-in. broad, lance-shaped and pointed leaves particularly attractive in the cream and green var. *variegata*. It may be grown as a trailing plant or a climber with support, but needs rather warm and moist conditions as its origins suggest. This also seems to be the place to mention *F. benjamina*, an Indian Fig, which grows with a slender stem and many thin drooping branches which carry long, ovate, leathery leaves of up to 4 in. and 1½ in. across, and forms a graceful weeping plant, with support for the central main stem. The culture of these figs is similar to that suggested for the upright-growing species, though for the last two a minimum of 55°F (13°C) is preferable, and both over-watering and drought should be avoided.

Fittonia

Family ACANTHACEAE

Fittonia argyroneura

Three Peruvian species of evergreen perennials compose this genus, distinctive for their beautifully marked and coloured foliage. *F. argyroneura* is typically a dwarf trailing plant with heart-shaped roundish oval leaves of 3 to 4 in. long, 2 to 3 in. wide, which are strikingly bright green, and netted with ivory-white veins. On *F. verschaffeltii*, of similar habit, the leaves are dark green with deep red veining, though there is a var. *pearcei* with leaves of lighter green with a light carmine network. Both plants can be grown as small pot plants trailing their stems over the sides, or as surface cover for larger plants such as palms. The flowers are insignificant and should be pinched out. The third species, *F. gigantea*, grows taller to 18 in. with broadly ovate leaves netted carmine-red. A peaty compost suits these plants which are most at home in shade, with warmth and humidity, being watered and sprayed freely in summer, moderately in winter, with a minimum temperature of 55°F (13°C) and no draughts. Propagate by cuttings of firm shoots in March, bottom heat of 75°F (23°C).

Bridal Wreath: Maiden's Wreath

Francoa   Family SAXIFRAGACEAE

Since their introduction from Chile in the 1830s, the three perennial species of herbs of this genus have been popular pot plants. *F. ramosa*, Maiden's Wreath, is a neat plant to use in groups, with lyre-shaped leaves and elegant sprays of white, four-petalled flowers on 2- to 3-ft stems in summer. In *F. sonchifolia*, Bridal Wreath, growth is not quite so tall and the flowers are pink, darkening to the centre; and in *F. appendiculata* leaves are longer stalked and the flowers deeper pink to red. Half-hardy plants like the

Francoa sonchifolia

sun and ample moisture. Being perennial, plants may be kept from year to year, winter temperature 45°F (7°C), with very moderate watering, but it is simpler to raise new plants from seeds sown in early spring (bottom heat 60°F (15·5°C), and grow on in JIP No. 2 compost in the greenhouse or plant room to begin flowering about July.

Lady's Ear Drops

Family ONAGRACEAE

Fuchsia

Fuchsia hybrida

These shrubs from Central and South America provide many delightful plants for indoors, attractive for their pendant flowers borne from the leaf axils singly or in clusters, and *F. fulgens*, Mexico, with long tubular scarlet flowers in leafy clusters; *F. splendens*, Mexico, with bright red, green-petalled flowers; and *F. triphylla*, San Domingo, with red to scarlet flowers in racemes, make good pot shrubs flowering in summer. Among the many hybrids 'Lustre', creamy-white tube and sepals, salmon-pink corolla flowers; 'Duke of York', cerise, bluish-violet; and 'Mr Rundle', pale rose, orange-vermilion, are good singles. 'Abbé Farges', cerise, rosy-lilac; 'Dainty Lady', cerise, white; 'Heritage', crimson, violet; 'Lena', flesh pink, purple; and 'Pink Ballet Girl', carmine, pink, are double-flowering. Pot or re-pot in March, JIP No. 3 compost, to grow in partial shade and temperature of 55° to 65°F (13° to 18°C), increasing water gradually. Feed fortnightly when buds show; after flowering, reduce watering; after leaf-fall, keep almost dry in frost-proof conditions (45°F (7°C)) through the winter. Propagate by cuttings of young, heeled shoots April to June inserted in pots, temperature 65°F (18°C).

Cape Jasmine

Gardenia

Family RUBIACEAE

Although there are some sixty distinctive evergreen shrubs in the genus, the one chiefly grown is *G. jasminoides*, which makes a pleasing shrub, when pot-grown, of 1 to 3 ft, with glossy, bright green, lance-shaped leaves, esteemed for its highly scented, white, salver-shaped flowers, borne to the ends of shoots, in late summer and autumn. There is a double-flowering form, and

Gardenia jasminoides

several bearing larger flowers than the type such as *fortuniana*. The plants are not very difficult to grow if certain points are watched. Potted in March, JIP No. 2 without the lime content, watered freely in summer with temperatures of 65° to 80°F (18° to 26·5°C), frequently syringed and leaves sponged, and then wintered with a minimum temperature of 50°F (10°C) with moderate watering, plants may be kept in health for up to three years after which flowering performance falls off and it is wise to replace. Good light and airy conditions without direct sun are needed at all times. Plants may be pruned to shape in February-March each year, and the top inch or so of compost renewed. Propagate by cuttings of young shoots 2 to 3 in. long inserted in JIC compost in February-April, bottom heat 75°F (23°C).

Gasteria

Family LILIACEAE

Gasteria verrucosa

Gasteria

All natives of South Africa, the forty known species of this genus are attractive, evergreen foliage plants, mainly stemless, with tongue-shaped, thick succulent leaves that often produce small, bell-shaped, hanging flowers on tall stems. They make good window plants in the house. Those readily available include *G. verrucosa*, sometimes called the Cape Hart's Tongue, with two-ranked, narrow-pointed leaves of grey-green, heavily covered with crowded white tubercles and scarlet and green flowers; *G. maculata* with leaves of dark green, twisted, and up to 8 in. long, with paler blotches of light green, and scarlet flowers on a very tall stem of 3 ft or more; *G. pulchra* with very narrow, tapering, glossy dark green leaves, having long white blotches on them, and scarlet flowers; and *G. liliputana*, a dwarf with pointed leaves, up to 2 in. long, dark green with much spotting with white markings and red flowers. A porous compost as for cacti or JIP No. 1 suits these plants, with regular watering in summer and a sunny position, while in winter only sparing watering is needed with a minimum temperature of 45° to 50°F (7° to 10°C). Propagate by leaf cuttings, or offsets, in spring.

Gesneria

Family GESNERIACEAE

This South American genus provides tuberous-rooted herbaceous plants which make a handsome show of fine crenulated foliage and spikes of colourful drooping, tubular flowers in summer. *G. (Rechsteineria) cardinalis* has large, heart-shaped and rounded velvety leaves, and bears many rich scarlet, tubular flowers in panicles, 2 ft tall, and *G. donkelaeriana*, with handsome, heart-shaped leaves of soft green tinged purple and red, and bright vermilion flowers on stems

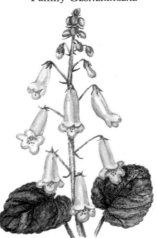

Gesneria cardinalis

of 18 to 24 in., is very rewarding, and there are hybrid forms with various flower colours, white, pink, orange and yellow. Tubers may be potted from March to June for a succession of bloom, JIP No. 2 compost, and need to be grown in a humid, warm atmosphere (65° to 85°F (18° to 29°C)), in good light but out of direct sun; syringing is not needed, but plants benefit by being on saucers of pebbles or gravel kept wet. After flowering, water is gradually withheld, and when the foliage dies the plants dried off and stored on their sides in a temperature not less than 50°F (10°C) until re-potting time. Propagate by leaf cuttings in summer, by young shoots in spring, or by seeds, with temperatures of 75° to 85°F (23 to 29°C).

Silk-Bark Oak

Family PROTEACEAE

Grevillea robusta

There are, it is recorded, some 230 species in this genus of evergreen trees and shrubs, native to Australia and New Zealand, but only a few make useful house plants. The chief is *G. robusta* delightful for its double-pinnate, fern-like leaves often more than 12 in. long, of a silky, bronzy-green on a single stem that makes an elegant foliage plant for any airy room. In nature it towers to 100 ft high; as a pot plant it can reach to 6 ft or more but takes a number of years in doing so. *G. thelemanniana* is a shrub form of 2 to 3 ft high with small pinnate leaves, and sometimes grown for its terminal racemes of pink and green tubular flowers in summer. Grevilleas are easy to grow, given JIP No. 2 compost, regular watering from spring onward, with a temperature of 65°F (18°C), and more moderate watering in winter with a minimum temperature of 50°F (10°C). New plants of *G. robusta* are best raised from seed in early spring, JIS compost, bottom heat of 65°F (18°C). Shrub species can be propagated from cuttings of ripe side shoots inserted in porous compost, temperature 65°F (18°C).

Guzmania

Family BROMELIACEAE

Guzmania

Only a few of the some eighty species of this genus of South American and West Indian stemless perennial epiphytic plants are in cultivation as house plants. They are interesting for their typical vase-like rosette of linear leaves and their flower spikes and colourfully bracted flowers appearing in summer. The most easily grown are *G. sanguinea* with pointed, lance-shaped leaves, tinged bright red along the edges and flowers of

Guzmania monostachya

yellowish-white with red bracts; *G zahnii*, a native of Costa Rica, growing 18 in. high, with long, sword-like leaves up to 20 in., brightly coloured yellow with crimson stripes, and a large flower spike of pale yellow flowers, short-lived individually, but numerous and quite effective; and *G. monostachya* (syn. *G. tricolor*) with a rosette of linear sword-like leaves 18 in. long, and flowers borne on a scape of 1 to 2 ft tall which are pure white, with bright pale yellow-green bracts streaked blackish-purple and tipped red, a type having a number of varieties. Their culture calls for a rich organic compost (see *Aechmea*), liberal watering, partial shade, summer warmth of about 65° to 70°F (18° to 21°C) and a minimum temperature in winter of 55°F (13°C) when watering should be regular but moderate. Propagate by offshoots at almost any time.

Blood Flower

Family AMARYLLIDACEAE *Haemanthus*

Haemanthus katherinae

South and Central Africa contributes this genus of fifty species of large bulbous plants with broad tough leaves and stout, thickish stems that bear at their heads striking umbels of richly coloured flowers in a dense well-stamened ball. *H. multiflorus* bears its large dense heads of deep red flowers on stalks of up to 2 ft in spring, with broad, oblong leaves of 12 in. or so; *H. katherinae* follows with beautiful heads of orange-salmon flowers in summer, together with the white-flowering *H. albiflorus*; while *H. coccineus*, flowering in September, carries its scarlet flowers in advance of its leaves. These are the most adaptable species in the house. The bulbs should be potted as available when about to make new growth, in JIP No. 3 compost, in pots just large enough to accommodate them, and be left undisturbed for three to four years. They like warmth (60° to 65°F (15·5 to 18°C)), regular watering and fortnightly feeding when coming into bloom; after flowering, water is gradually withheld, and when foliage yellows, the bulbs are kept dry with minimum winter temperature of 50°F (10°C) until new growth begins. Propagate by offsets when re-potting, spring-flowering kinds in October-November, autumn-flowering in March-April.

Hamatocactus

Hamatocactus

Family CACTACEAE

The few species of this genus of Cacti are native to Texas and Mexico, where they are known as Strawberry Cacti on account of their strawberry-like fruit. The fruits are unlikely to form under house cultivation, but *H. setispinus* is attractive for its long, dark green body, with thin, high ribs, wavy-edged and set with many white and brown radial spines, flowering

Hamatocactus setispinus

freely when mature, with funnel-shaped yellow, red-centred flower at the top. *H. hamatacanthus* with spiralling ribs and bright red spines bears similar flowers. These plants are happy in light or partial shade, with moderate watering in summer, little in winter, when the temperature should not fall below 50°F (10°C) for their comfort. Propagate by seed.

Haworthia

Family LILIACEAE

Haworthia attenuata

Many of these plants from South Africa make interesting and easily contented house plants. All are stemless, but some form rosettes of their succulent leaves, others grow them overlapping and columnar. Their attraction lies in their foliage, for the flowers borne in long racemes on slender stems are inconspicuous. Some of the best for windowsills are: *H. chalwinii*, columnar with erect, thick leaves, spirally arranged, with white tubercles along the back, to 6 to 8 in. high; *H. coarctata*, similar with slender-pointed leaves: *H. fasciata*, with rosettes of spreading shiny green, white-banded leaves; *H. margaritifera*, rosettes of erect, incurving leaves, grey-green with many pearly-white tubercles; *H. sessiliflora*, with clusters of thick, pointed, pale green leaves with translucent lines; *H. tessellata*, with short, thick, recurving dark translucent leaves, with lighter markings, in simple rosettes; and *H. truncata*, a 'window' plant, interesting for its abruptly flat, translucent top to its ovalish, dull green, rosetted leaves. A simple porous compost (JIP No. 1) will suit, with positions in partial shade, moderate watering in summer and occasional watering in winter, with a minimum temperature of 50°F (10°C). Propagate by offsets in spring.

Hechtia

Family BROMELIACEAE

Although there are some thirty species in this genus of Mexican perennials, they have as yet received little attention and only one is much grown. This is *H. argentea*, a striking foliage plant with sharply recurved, rigid spiny leaves about 12 in. long, produced in a dense rosette and beautifully silvered on both sides. The white flowers pro-

Hechtia argentea

duced in rounded clusters on a tall spike are rather insignificant though in keeping with the appearamce of the plant. A porous compost as for Aechmea (q.v.) suits, with a position in good light, moderate watering, and spraying of the leaves in summer; occasional watering in winter, with a minimum temperature of 50°F (10°C). Propagate by offsets.

Ivy

Family ARALIACEAE *Hedera*

Hedera helix

The evergreen climbers valued for their foliage are largely varieties of two species, the hardy *H. helix*, native to Britain and Europe, and the less hardy *H. canariensis* of the Azores and Canary Islands. *H. helix* varieties are: *cristata* interesting for its small leaves, fringed at the edges; *lutzii* with very tiny leaves, mottled lime and yellow; but for variegated leaves, the named forms are best, such as 'Chicago', emerald green; 'Glacier', silvery blue-green with creamy-white margins; 'Golden Jubilee', golden in the centre; and 'Pittsburgh', deep green. The Irish Ivy, *H. hibernica*, has a yellow-variegated form in *maculata*, and var. *marmorata*, with marbled green and cream leaves. *H. canariensis* provides two outstanding forms in var. *foliis variegatis* with cream-edged leaves, and 'Golden Leaf'. By pinching out the leading shoots above a node as necessary, the plants are kept compact. Potted in March, JIP No. 3 compost, and re-potted every three or four years, given partial shade or light, with liberal watering in summer, moderate in winter, and a minimum temperature of 45°F (7°C), plants thrive for many years. Propagate by cuttings in autumn, with bottom heat of 55° to 60°F (13° to 15·5 C).

Rose Mallow

Hibiscus

Family MALVACEAE

Containing herbs, shrubs and trees, this genus of about 150 species provides a lovely shrub which will succeed in heated plant rooms in *H. rosa-sinensis*, the Chinese Rose Mallow, which grows up to about 4 ft when pot-grown, with ovate, coarsely-toothed shiny leaves, and large, mallow flowers, up to 5 in. across from the leaf axils in summer. In the species, these are bright rose-red, but there are several beautiful varieties of various shades of white, pink to red, in

Hibiscus rosa-sinensis

semi-double and double flowering forms, to be had from specialist growers. There is also a var. *cooperi* valued for its beautifully variegated foliage which is a bright green ground colour marked with olive-green, cream, white and crimson blotches and a carmine edging. Plants are best grown in large pots, JIP No. 3 compost, watered freely from March to October with summer temperature of 65° to 70°F (18° to 21°C), and only moderate watering in winter with minimum temperature of 55°F (13°C). Plants may be kept shapely by pruning back straggling growth in February. Propagate by cuttings of firm young shoots, spring or summer, in JIC compost, bottom heat 70°F (21°C).

Barbados Lily: Equestrian Star

Family AMARYLLIDACEAE *Hippeastrum*

Hippeastrum aulicum

Bulbous plants, gorgeous in flower, sometimes placed under *Amaryllis*. Under cool conditions they flower in spring and early summer, but in heated conditions may be had in flower early in the New Year. Species growing are: *H. aulicum* of Brazil, which bears its large, funnel-shaped flowers of rich crimson, purple and green at the base, on 12- to 18-in. stalks; *H. equestre* var. *splendens* is a brilliant red; *H. pardinum*, Peru, has flowers of rich cream dotted with crimson, over 6 in. across; and *H. patense*, Chile, with three to four bright scarlet, feathered yellow, flowers. There is an even wider range of colours in the named hybrids and forms. Bulbs are potted in winter to early spring, JIP No. 3, with repotting once every three to four years, and watered moderately until in growth, and then freely until after flowering, when watering is continued, with temperature of 60°F (15·5 °C). In summer, plants can be placed in a cold frame or greenhouse after flowering. By September, growth will be completed and less water needed until about October when the bulbs should be rested under cool conditions (50°F (10°C)) until restarted into growth. Propagate by offsets when re-potting.

Hovea

Hovea

Family LEGUMINOSAE

Hovea celsii

From Australia and Tasmania, these near-hardy evergreen shrubs include *H. celsii* which grows 2 to 4 ft high when pot-grown with narrow, blunt-ended, alternate leaves out of the axils of which are borne leafy-stalked clusters of blue pea-like flowers, freely, in early spring. *H. chorizemifolia* of 1 to 4 ft has small, spine-toothed leaves somewhat like those of holly, and intense blue and white flowers about April or May; and *H. longifolia* with narrow, pointed linear leaves, has blue-purple flowers in June, but may grow to 8 ft tall in time. Airy conditions suit these plants best, with good light, and gradually increasing watering in spring. After flowering they can be re-potted, and in July to September placed outside plunged in ashes or soil in a warm sheltered place; to be brought indoors to conditions of a minimum temperature in winter of about 50°F (10°C), given moderate watering only, and very little in November to January. JIP No. 2 compost suits the plants, and any pruning necessary can be done after flowering. Propagate by cuttings of firm young shoots in spring (bottom heat 60°F (15·5°C)). Or may be raised from seeds, temrature 55°F (13°C).

Curly Palm: Thatch Leaf Palm

Family PALMACEAE   *Howea*

Howea belmoreana

Both species of this genus are very attractive palms for the house with feather-like, finely divided foliage. Native to Lord Howe's Island in the South Pacific, they require frost-proof quarters at least and are satisfactory in heated rooms. At one time listed under *Kentia* they are still sold commercially as Kentia palms. *H. belmoreana* is known as the Curly Palm since its leaf segments droop archingly; under pot growth it reaches 6 to 10 ft in several years; *H. forsteriana* is similar but the leaves are flatter and the leaf segments fewer, and it is known as the Flat Palm or Thatch Leaf Palm. They need minimum summer temperature of about 55°F (13°C) and winter 50°F (10°C), but grow quite happily under greater warmth, with freely given watering in summer and moderate watering October to March. Leaves benefit from spraying and sponging often. Pot in February or March, repotting when the roots really fill the pots, JIP No. 3 compost. Propagate if the urge is there by seeds, which must be freshly ripe, in spring, bottom heat 75°F (23°C).

Hoya Family ASCLEPIADACEAE

The majority of the evergreen shrubs, numbering about seventy, of this genus belong to Malaysia, but the one species worth growing as a house plant, *H. carnosa*, comes from Queensland, Australia. It is a delightful evergreen climbing plant, capable of growing to 10ft, easily managed, and becoming more beautiful with age. Although it can put out aerial

Hoya carnosa

roots like Ivy, it is best trained up a support or trellis or by a window, where it will display its smooth, somewhat fleshy, oval, pointed dark green leaves, and loose, hanging clusters of wax-like, starry, pinkish-white flowers on slender stalks, for several weeks in summer. Potted in March, JIP No. 3 compost, it requires a summer temperature of 55° to 65°F (13° to 18°C) with liberal watering, and a winter temperature of about 50°F (10°C) with very moderate watering. Weak shoots may be cut back in February, and growth thinned if necessary, but the spurs or foot stalks that remain after flowering should be left intact as they will produce fresh flowers. Propagate by cuttings of the previous year's shoots, 4 in. long, in spring or early summer, bottom heat 75°F (23°C), or by layering.

Hyacinth

Family LILIACEAE   *Hyacinthus*

Hyacinthus orientalis

The genus is monotypic, *H. orientalis*, native to Italy and countries east to Asia Minor, from which the modern cultivated florists' hyacinths have been developed. The plants fall into two groups: the early-flowering Roman Hyacinths (*H. orientalis* var. *albulus* of Southern France) and the large-flowered Common or Dutch Hyacinths. Roman Hyacinths have scented white flowers, are potted in August to flower in December or January. The large-flowered hyacinth bulbs are available in September to November. The flower is a crowded spike of wax-like, bell-shaped flowers, in a range of colours of white, blue, yellow, pink and red, and specialists' lists should be consulted for named varieties. Bulbs may be potted in JIP compost or in bulb fibre (moist peat fibre, plus crushed oyster shell and charcoal, about 5 per cent of each), watered and then placed in a cold frame or sheltered place out of doors or in a cold cellar or dark cupboard, until shoot growth is well forward, and then brought into the light, in cool rooms, with a final move after a week or two to where they are to flower (60° to 65°F (15·5° to 18°C)), with good light, ventilation and moderate watering.

Hydrangea

Family SAXIFRAGACEAE

Many lovely flowering shrubs may be chosen from *H. macrophylla* and its forms. Native to Japan the plants make excellent pot subjects bearing huge, rounded heads of sterile bracted flowers in various hues of white, pink, red, purple and blue, at the ends of shoots, against bright green foliage and may be had in flower from July to September. Good named forms are; 'Mme. E. Mouillère', white; 'Générale Vicomtesse de Vibraye', blue; 'Hamburg', pink; 'Ami Pasquier', crimson (or deep blue); 'La Marne', pink (or blue); 'Vulcain', salmon red (or deep blue); 'Niedersachen', pale pink (or pale blue); and 'Westfalen', crimson-purple. Pot in February-March in rich compost, JIP No. 3 is suitable, but for blue-flowering the loam must be lime-free. Intensity of blueness can be increased by adding aluminium sulphate to the compost (four to six ounces per bushel). Light, airy conditions without direct sun, liberal watering and fortnightly feeding when coming into flower are the chief needs, with temperatures of 60° to 65°F (15·5° to 18°C). After flowering, plants may stand out of doors. Propagate by cuttings of young shoots of three to four nodes in May, or of unflowered ripe shoots 6 to 8 in. long in August.

Hydrangea macrophylla

Balsam: Busy Lizzie

Family BALSAMINACEAE

Impatiens

Impatiens holstii

Of this genus the half-hardy annual, *I. balsamina* and its forms, hailing from India and Malaysia, is much appreciated as a pot plant and its rapid growth has earned it the sobriquet of 'Busy Lizzie'. Of long, free-flowering habit, it has several varieties, from the dwarf bushy forms such as 'Orange Baby', 'Salmon Rose' etc. to the beautiful double-camillia-flowered vars. in a variety of bright colours. Plants may be bought or grown from seeds, in JI composts (temperature 65° to 75°F (18° to 23°C)), in spring. Indoors a light, airy and sunny position is admirable, with liberal watering, occasional pinching out of shoots to keep bushy, and the taller kinds benefit from staking for their brittle stems. *I. holstii* is a half-hardy perennial relative from Eastern tropical Africa, making a larger plant, but with beautiful, spurred bright scarlet flowers, in a branching plant growing 2 ft or so tall, and there are hybrids yielding compact plants with flowers of an exquisite range of colours. Plants are potted and re-potted in spring, JIP No. 3 compost, and require similar summer treatment to *I. balsamina*; in winter, very moderate watering with minimum temperature of 55°F (13°C) is needed. Propagate by seeds or cuttings of strong shoots in summer.

Incarvillea

Incarvillea

Family BIGNONIACEAE

Incarvillea

Largely native to China and Tibet this genus of about seven species of smooth - textured herbaceous perennials with fine pinnate foliage and large tubular flowers yields an excellent pot plant in *I. delavayi*, handsome for its radical, dark green leaves, and large Gloxinia-like, trumpet flowers of crimson-purple with yellow-veined throats produced in clusters on 18-in. stems; var. 'Bees' Pink' is excellent with very large pale pink flowers; *I. mairei* (*grandiflora*) is more dwarf, with only one or two flowers per stem, but they

Incarvillea delavayi

are up to 4 in. across, and in var. *brevipes* a brilliant crimson. Potted in spring, JIP No. 3 compost, the plants may be grown under light, airy conditions in cool rooms to flower in June-July, temperatures of about 60° to 65°F (15.5° to 18°C). After flowering, plants which are near hardy may be placed out of doors plunged in ashes or the soil, and may remain there with winter frost-protection of cloches or a cold frame or even organic litter, until wanted for indoor flowering again. Propagate by seeds in spring, temperature 65°F (18°C), or by root division when re-potting every fourth year.

Violet Cress

Family CRUCIFERAE

Ionopsidium

Ionopsidium acaule

Known popularly as Violet Cress or Diamond Flower, the only species commonly grown of this two-species genus, *I. acaule* is a delightfully attractive, neat-growing, tufted annual, ideal to grow in pots or pans for shady window-sills where it will quickly spread its small rounded or orb-shaped leaves to cover them and raise its four-petalled lilac or white, stained violet flowers on 2- to 3-in. stems. This pretty plant from Portugal is easily raised from seeds sown very shallowly in pots or pans filled with JIP No. 1 compost in September for early flowering next year, in April for summer flowering, thinning the seedlings to 1 in. apart. Over-wintered plants need only cool conditions, temperature of about 50°F (10°C), with moderate watering. Flowering is prolific, and may be encouraged by feeding when flower buds show, and fortnightly until they are getting over.

Moon Flower

Ipomoea

Family CONVOLVULACEAE

Of this large genus of over 300 species of climbing, twining plants, *I. horsfalliae* of the West Indies is a magnificent perennial climber with handsome, five-fingered, evergreen leaves of lance-shaped, wavy-edged leaflets, and gorgeous, rich rose, funnel-shaped flowers with petals opening full in winter; it can be grown under central-heated conditions where light and humidity are assured. Its var. *briggsii* is even better, flowering more

Ipomoea horsfalliae

freely with magenta-crimson flowers. Potted in an 8- or 10-in. pot, JIP No. 3, it grows to 8 to 10 ft requiring supports or light trellis on which it may be trained, by a window or in a plant room, with winter temperatures of 55° to 65°F (13° to 18°C), moderate watering; prune straggling growth after flowering, top-dress the soil, and water more freely April to September when the plant makes an ornamental foliage subject. Propagate by layering in summer, or in the case of var. *briggsii* by stem cuttings in spring or summer, bottom heat 75°F (23°C).

Ixora: Indian Jasmine

Family RUBIACEAE

Ixora

Ixora coccinea

Tropical shrubs of colourful, showy flowers and attractive evergreen foliage that are easy to cultivate and some are adaptable to house conditions where there is central heating. The flowers are borne in large terminal heads or corymbs in summer against foliage of opposite, leathery, glossy green leaves. *I. coccinea* of the East Indies has flower clusters of bright red 5 to 6 in. across, and has orange-scarlet flowering vars. in *pilgrimii* and *morsei*. *I. chinensis* is a fine compact shrub with light orange flowers, and white, pink, yellow and deeper orange varieties. Beautiful hybrids include *I.* × *chelsonii* with orange-salmon and pink flowers; *I.* × *decora*, yellow and rose; and *I.* × *splendida*, orange-crimson. Potted in a porous but peaty compost (four parts by volume fibrous peat, one part loam, one part sharp sand) in February-March, plants like shade, warmth and humidity, with day temperatures up to 75°F (23°C) and night not less than 60°F (15·5°C), with increasing watering, and daily syringing; feed weekly from coming into bud. After flowering, watering should be moderate, and for the winter drier conditions and lower temperatures (55° to 65°F (13° to 18°C)) should prevail. Propagate by cuttings of firm young shoots in spring, bottom heat 75° to 85°F (23° to 29°C).

Mimosa-Leaved Ebony Tree

Jacaranda
Family BIGNONIACEAE

The fifty or so species in this genus of tropical American shrubs and trees resemble some of the Acacia or Mimosa in their attractive finely cut foliage and habit, but their flowers are tubular and quite distinctive. *J. mimosifolia* (syn. *J. ovalifolia*), native to Brazil, is chiefly grown, and makes a delightful pot plant when young, with double-pinnate, fern-like foliage of light green, and when well established bearing beautiful lavender-blue drooping

Jacaranda mimosifolia

tubular flowers in loose, upright pyramidal panicles in summer; there is a white form, *alba*. Even when not in flower it is ornamental, though growing large eventually to about 6 to 10 ft but can be kept shapely by pruning after flowering. Potted in February-March, JIP No. 2 compost, it welcomes warmth (70° to 75°F. (21° to 23°C)) with humidity and increasing watering, spraying daily in summer; but from September, cooler conditions should prevail, and a drier atmosphere in winter, with only moderate watering and a minimum temperature of 55°F (13°C). Propagate by cuttings of firm shoots in summer, bottom heat 75°F (23°C), under glass.

Jasmine: Jessamine

Family OLEACEAE

Jasminum

Jasminum polyanthum

Jasmines are a flowering genus of the Olive family, with species scattered about the temperate, sub-tropical and tropical parts of the world. The most useful as a house plant is the Chinese *J. polyanthum*, a twining climber, best known for its pinnate dark green leaves and many-flowered panicles of highly scented, star-like flowers, white inside and flushed rosy-pink outside, borne in February to April. It is best grown on a light trellis, and kept compact by pinching out the growing points of new shoots as they appear from spring to October, and then letting the plant grow on to flower. After flowering, a plant may be pruned more drastically. *J. grandiflorum* of the Himalayas is evergreen with clusters of white flowers, reddish outside, from June to October, to be kept neat with judicious pruning after flowering. Potted in March, JIP No. 2 compost, with watering regulated by active growth, and well-lighted, airy positions, these plants will succeed under minimum winter temperatures of 50° to 55°F (10° to 13°C). Propagate by cuttings of firm shoots in spring and summer; bottom heat of about 70°F (21°C).

Kalanchoe

Family CRASSULACEAE

Kalanchoe

The genus is one of half-hardy succulent plants, found chiefly in tropical countries. The most successful as a house pot plant is *K. blossfeldiana*, a small shrub of not more than 12 in. high from Madagascar producing many stems with dark green notched leaves, edged red, and panicles of small orange-red flowers with a sweet scent, in the winter months. Its compatriots, *K. beharensis*, with stems up to 2 or 3 ft and large, heart-shaped, toothed leaves, rust-red with fine hairs in youth

Kalanchoe blossfeldiana

turning white later; and *K. tomentosa*, 18 in., with thick small ovalish leaves with silvery hairs giving a plush-like feel, and rust-red at the tip of the leaves, are grown purely for their foliage for they do not flower. *K. marmorata* of Abyssinia is grown for its roundish notched leaves which are grey-green, waxy and with brown marking, and its large white flowers in spring. Potted in March, JIP No. 3 compost, plants need cool, light and airy conditions with free watering in summer, moderate in winter and a minimum temperature of about 50°F (10°C). Propagate by seeds in spring, bottom heat 60° to 65°F (15·5° to 18°C), or by cuttings of shoots in summer, 2 to 3 in. long, allowed to callus in the air for a day or two before insertion.

Candle Plant

Family COMPOSITAE   *Kleinia*

Kleinia articulata

Sometimes included in *Senecio* to which it is closely related, this genus of succulent sub-shrubs of perhaps twenty species, natives of the Canary Islands and South Africa, provides an unusual plant for the house in *K. articulata* which grows with erect, round, jointed, glaucous-blue stems, covered by a grey, waxy bloom that earn it the name of Candle Plant. It grows in winter producing small leaves that soon wither, and long-stemmed corymbs of yellowish-white flowers. *K. neriifolia* from the Canary Islands is interesting for its branching upright growth of waxy cylindrical stems, at the end of which spiky, linear leaves 6 in. long are produced in winter in rosettes, to fall in spring, and corymbs of yellowish-white flowers in autumn. These plants should receive as much light as possible, with a minimum temperature in winter of 45°F (7°C), moderate once-a-week watering in winter, and a brief rest after flowering. Propagate by cuttings in summer.

Jamaica Mountain Sage

Lantana

Family VERBENACEAE

Out of the fifty tropical shrubs of this genus, a few make pleasing ever-green flowering plants when grown in pots, and as such are decoratively eligible for the house. They are distinctive for their round heads of flowers which change as they age, so that a plant may have flowers in three colours at the same time. *L. camara* of Jamaica and the East Indies has flowers of pink or yellow changing to orange or red in sum-mer, from the axils of

Lantana camara

opposite, oval, pointed leaves, downy beneath, and has several varietal and hybrid forms in different flower tints. From South Africa comes *L. salvifolia* with aromatic leaves and lilac or pink flowers; and *L. selloviana* has trailing or procumbent stems, with rosy lilac flowers for some time. Plants may be raised from seeds sown early in the year to flower in six months or so, and then discarded; but if over-wintered, with moderate watering, temperature of 50°F (10°C), pruned in February and grown on, they flower the more freely. Light, airy conditions, liberal watering and summer temperatures of 55° to 65°F (13° to 18°C) suit these plants. Propagate by cuttings of firm shoots in August and September, temperature of 65°F (18°C).

131

Chilean Bell-Flower

Family LILIACEAE   *Lapageria*

Lapageria rosea

The one species of this genus is a near-hardy twining evergreen climbing shrub from Chile, *L. rosea*, with handsome, broad-based, ovate, leathery, dark green, alternate leaves, out of the axils of which appear clusters of large, pretty, bell-shaped, waxy, rose-crimson flowers about 3 in. long, during summer; in var. *superba* the flowers are particularly large and bright rich crimson, and in var. *albiflora*, a clear white. Potted in March in a peaty compost (three parts by volume fibrous peat, one part loam, one part sharp sand, with a little charcoal), and grown, with support up which to twine, in well-lighted, humid, but cool conditions, in a plant room or conservatory, or by a large window, a plant needs fairly heavy watering, daily spraying, and will grow 6 to 8 ft from an 8-in. pot, often flowering from late July into autumn. Only very moderate watering is needed in October to March, with a minimum temperature of 45° to 50°F (7° to 10°C). Rather susceptible to insects, such as mealy bug, thrips and scale, which are best anticipated by applying a systemic insecticide. Propagate by seeds, bottom heat 65°F (18°C) or by layering strong shoots in spring or autumn.

Lion's Tail: Lion's Ear

Leonotis

Family LABIATAE

This genus of some thirty species of African shrubs and herbs may be drawn upon for an outstanding, winter-flowering, half-hardy shrub in *L. leonurus*, which may be grown in an 8-in. pot to make a shapely bush of up to 3 ft or more, with lance-shaped, narrow, downy leaves, form the opposite axils of which appear bright orange-scarlet, tubular flowers with two spreading lips, in showy whorls, in October to December; there is also a good white-flowering var. *albiflora*. Potted in March or April, JIP

Leonotis leonurus

No. 3 compost, plants need airy, light conditions, with moderate watering and temperatures of 55° to 65°F (13° to 18°C). After flowering, growth should be pruned to shape, and the plants wintered with very occasional watering in a minimum temperature of 45°F (7°C) while dormant. If pressed for space, plants may be plunged in ashes out of doors in a sheltered sunny place from June to September and then brought in for flowering. Propagate by cuttings of firm young shoots in spring, or by seeds (bottom heat of 65°F (18°C)).

Japanese Honeysuckle

Family CAPRIFOLIACEAE

Lonicera

Lonicera japonica
var. *aureo, reticulata*

The honeysuckle genus embraces about 180 bushy or climbing shrubs, natives of various parts of the Northern Hemisphere. For the house, however, the most charming and successful is the golden variegated-leaved *L. japonica* var. *aureoreticulata*, preferably grown as a young plant. It is an evergreen twining climber, less vigorous than the type, with its reddish shoots carrying opposite, broadly ovate and pointed leaves in which the mid-ribs and veins are of bright yellow, and a well-grown specimen makes a glowing ornamental picture at any time of the year. Potted in autumn, JIP No. 3 compost, and given a light, airy position, with sparing watering and a minimum temperature of 45°F (7°C) in winter, the plant makes new growth in the spring, and then requires gradually increasing water supplies, and good light to bring out the variegation. New growths can be pinched back to keep the plant bushy, but some support should be given, or shoots allowed to twine up a trellis. Propagate by layering in spring or summer, or cuttings of firm shoots in August.

Creeping Jenny

Lysimachia

Family PRIMULACEAE

Of this genus of over 100 species of herbaceous perennials, *L. nummularia*, commonly called Creeping Jenny and native to Britain and mid-Europe, is often grown as a pot plant or basket plant for indoors being esteemed for bright yellow, starlike flowers, produced singly but freely from the leaf-axils of shortstalked, roundish, fresh green leaves from June to September; it has a var. *aurea* with goldenyellow leaves, rather less robust growing. Potted in March, JIP No. 2 compost, plants will

Lysimachia nummularia

flourish in shade or light, but not direct sun, and may be watered freely. The prostrate stems grow out 12 in. or more, but may have the tips pinched out to keep the plant more bushy. After flowering, plants may be kept under quite cool conditions, with very little water during the winter, or plunged out of doors in a sheltered spot. Propagate by division in March.

False Mallow

Family MALVACEAE

Malvastrum

Malvastrum × hypomadarum

The False Mallow has been long esteemed and cultivated as an indoor shrub of charming character, and is a hybrid, *M. × hypomadarum*, stemming from the parentage of two South African species, *M. capense × M. scabrosum*. Branching readily, with slender shoots, ovate, roughly-toothed leaves of $\frac{1}{2}$ to $1\frac{1}{2}$ in. long, it produces white, flushed pink and streaked deep purple, open-faced, five-petalled flowers on slender stalks, freely in summer, and being nearly hardy responds to straightforward culture. Potted in March, JIP No. 3 compost and given light, airy conditions with ample watering, it succeeds well. After flowering, it may be pruned to shape and wintered under frost-proof conditions (45°F (7°C) minimum), with soil just kept slightly moist. Propagate by cuttings of firm, young shoots in spring.

Arrowroot Plant: Prayer Plant

Maranta

Family MARANTACEAE

A genus of rhizomatous-rooted, tropical American perennials chiefly attactive for their ornamental foliage and suitability for heated rooms. The most popular is *M. leuconeura* var. *kerchoveana* of Brazil, with oblong, oval leaves on short stems, to about 12 in. high, of pale green with

Maranta leuconeura

darker blotches of purplish-red between the main veins and at the margins. At night the leaves tend to fold or curl inward and stand more upright, a habit that has led to its being called the Prayer Plant. Var. *massangeana* differs in having slightly smaller leaves, with the main veins tending to be ribbed and white. In *M. bicolor* the short-stemmed leaves grow to about 1 ft, the blades being broadly oblong about 6 in. long by 4 in. wide, dark green with lighter green blotches between the mid-rib and margins, and purplish beneath. A useful compost is three parts by volume sifted oak or beech leaf-mould, two parts moss peat, and one part coarse sand, with four ounces JIB fertilizer to each bushel. Plants are potted in April-May, watered freely in summer, grown in partial shade; moderate watering in autumn, and almost no water in December to March, with a winter temperature of not less than 55°F (13°C). Propagate by division in April when growth is just beginning.

Swiss Cheese Plant

Family ARACEAE *Monstera*

Monstera deliciosa

There are about thirty known species in this genus of tropical evergreen climbing plants found in the West Indies and nearby countries of tropical America, but as yet few are in cultivation. The best known is *M. deliciosa*, a native of Mexico, that grows with erect, thickish stems, equipped with aerial roots, and produces large, broadly ovate, thick, leathery leaves, up to 2 ft across, deeply cut or perforated, a shining apple green above, yellowish-green beneath, and can grow steadily to a considerable size. In America it is known as the Ceriman, and in nature bears a spadix of yellowish flowers that give way to succulent, edible fruits said to have a pineapple flavour. *M. pertusa* is a similar plant with somewhat smaller leaves, usually perforated irregularly, a characteristic that earns it the name of the Swiss Cheese Plant. For the house these plants may be grown in large pots, compost as for Maranta, and given airy conditions, though shade is quite welcome, in warm rooms, or halls, or foyers, with summer temperatures of 65° to 75°F (18° to 23°C), ample watering and spraying in warm weather, moderate but regular watering in winter with temperatures of 55° to 65°F (13° to 18°C). Propagate by stem cuttings, in JIC compost, bottom heat 75°F (23°C).

Daffodil

Narcissus
'Soleil D'Or'

Narcissus Family AMARYLLIDACEAE

Horticulturally these bulbous plants are divided into eleven divisions which are (with typical variety given): (1) Trumpet ('King Alfred'), (2) Large-cupped Narcissi ('Fortune'), (3) Small-cupped ('La Riante'), (4) Double ('Inglescombe'), (5) Triandrus ('Angel's Tears'), (6) Cyclamineus ('Peeping Tom'), (7) Jonquilla ('Golden Sceptre'), (8) Tazetta (Poetaz) ('Cheerfulness'), (9) Poeticus ('Actaea'), (10) Species and Wild Forms, (11) Miscellaneous. Some varieties lend themselves better to being grown in pots than others. Bulbs may be potted from August to November in JIP composts or prepared bulb fibre, kept cool in cold frame, cellar, or plunged in ashes, until shoot growth is showing (six to eight weeks) when plants are then brought to light and cool conditions (50°F (10°C)), and moved to where they are to flower. After flowering the plants should be watered until leaves are yellow, when they can be dried off or planted out of doors. The Polyanthus vars. 'Soleil D'Or' and 'Paperwhite' may be grown in fibre for Christmas, or in water wedged in pebbles. Propagate by offsets at potting time. Plants from seeds take three to six years to flower, but seeds may be sown in autumn.

139

Narcissus (Species)

Family AMARYLLIDACEAE

Narcissus cyclamineus

Apart from the florists' varieties of daffodils and narcissi, there are some very charming dwarf species which may be enjoyed in the house, provided they are not subject to forcing. *N. bulbocodium*, 6 in. tall, the yellow Hoop Petticoat Daffodil, with hooped cup and rush-like foliage, may be grown in variety; *N. cyclamineus*, 6 in., with its clear yellow, reflexed-petalled flowers; *N. juncifolius*, the rush-leaved Daffodil, 3 in., golden-yellow; *N. minimus*, 3 in., and its tiny trumpet flowers; *N. nanus*, 5 in., with sulpur yellow and cream trumpet flowers; *N. triandrus albus*, 7 in., the white Angel's Tears Daffodil, and its forms; and *N. watieri*, 4 in., with pure white flowers, are some of the kinds to seek. Potted early in August-September, JIP No. 2 compost, to be grown cool, in the dark until shoot tips are showing, and then in light, airy conditions with temperatures of about 50°F (10°C), until flowers are opening, when a little more warmth can be taken, these exquisite miniatures are excellent for cool rooms or window-sills. After flowering, they must be kept growing until the leaves wither, when the bulbs can be dried off, and later planted out, in rock garden or alpine lawn or cool position out of doors.

Ladder Fern

Nephrolepis

Family POLYPODIACEAE

There are some thirty-five species to this genus of tropical ferns, but the finest and most long-lived as a house plant is *N. exaltata*, with finely cut, pinnate fronds of up to 2 ft long and 6 in. broad, growing rapidly and requiring a fair amount of room. There are also several beautiful varieties of it, such as *elegantissima*, *magnifica* and *whitmanii*, in which the fronds are evenly, more finely cut and pinnately divided. Another useful plant is *N. cordifolia* var. *compacta*, excellent for pots, with deep glossy green, arching fronds, up to 2 ft long. Potted in March, using two

Nephrolepsis exaltata

parts by volume leaf-mould, one part sandy peat and one part sand, these ferns appreciate a summer temperature of 70°F (21°C), with shade and liberal watering, and a winter of 50°F (10°C) minimum, with more moderate watering. Propagate by division in March.

Bead Plant: Coral-Berried Duckweed

Family RUBIACEAE   *Nertera*

Nertera granadensis

Of the six small, creeping perennials from mountainous country of the warm temperate regions of the Southern Hemisphere, *N. granadensis* (syn. *N. depressa*) is a favourite window-sill plant for pots or pans. It is found in South America, New Zealand and Australia, a dwarf, mat-forming plant of about 3 in. high, with creeping stems, rooting as they go, packed with small, ovate, fleshy green leaves, with minute greenish flowers in their axils that give way to bright orange-scarlet round fruits or berries, set like beads among the foliage in summer and autumn. New Zealand contributes two other similar species, *N. balfouriana*, with rather broader leaves and berries more pear-shaped; and *N. cunninghamii*, with narrower leaves and more slender growth. Potted in March, JIP compost, the plants are happy under cool, light or shady conditions, well watered through the summer, then moderate watering only with a minimum winter temperature of 45°F (7°C). Propagate by division in spring; by seeds with bottom heat of 60°F (15·5°C).

Bird's Nest Bromeliad

Nidularium

Family BROMELIACEAE

This genus of epiphytic plants, native to Brazil, is characterized by the growth of linear, acutely-pointed and spiny leaves in rosette formation, in the centre of which the closely packed head of bracted flowers nestles. *N. innocentii* is easy to keep, growing with serrated linear leaves, up to about 12 in. long, 1½ to 2 in. wide, dark green above, reddish-purple beneath, and the cen-

Nidularium fulgens

tre of the rosette turns brilliant red, when the head of nondescript greenish-white flowers forms. *N. fulgens* is even more showy, with leaves in a dense rosette, about 12 in. long, and spreading, and mottled in shades of green, and the inner leaves a brilliant scarlet when the violet, white- and red-clustered head of flowers develops. *N. rutilans* has a rosette of rather broad, foot-long leaves, spotted dark green, and flowers of vermilion set amid bract leaves of shaded rose and red. Potted in spring, compost as for *Aechmea* (q.v.), these plants require even temperatures, summer 60° to 65°F (15·5° to 18°C), winter 50° to 55°F (10° to 13°C) with moderate watering only; in winter no more than the cup of the rosette will hold. Leaves should be sprayed or sponged to keep free from dust. Propagate by suckers or offsets as for *Aechmea*.

Indian Fig: Prickly Pear

Family CACTACEAE

Opuntia

With a habitat range reaching from Utah to the tip of South America, the cacti of this genus show variation, and are divided into sub-genera: (1) Cylindropuntia—plants having cylindrical stems, branching and jointed, of which *O. salmiana*, Brazil, Argentine, branches with thin, cylindrical joints, and flowers freely with yellow flowers; and *O subulata*, Argentine, grows tall, branching, with persistent leaves and long single spines. (2) Tephrocactus—plants having cylindrical or globose stems, but low-growing, of which *O. platyacantha*, Chile, prostrate with many flat, flexible papery spines, and *O. verschaffeltii* with soft stems, almost spineless, and reddish-purple, are worth growing. (3) Platyopuntia—plants having round or oval, flattened pads, which bear the fruit known as 'Prickly Pears'. Here *O. basilaris*, Nevada, Arizona, Utah, with broad, oval purplish pads, velvety with soft brown bristles (glochids), but spineless, and pinkish-purple flowers, and *O. microdasys*, spineless with white bristles, are representative. They are easily grown in a porous compost—JIP No. 1 will suit—with liberal watering in April to October, and sparing in winter, minimum temperature of 45° to 50°F (7° to 10°C). Propagate by cuttings.

Opuntia microdasys

Oxalis

Family OXALIDACEAE

This large genus of perennial herbs has a few which lend themselves admirably to pot culture for the house. *O. adenophylla* from Chile grows 4 to 6 in. high, from a bulb-like rhizome, with round, many-leafleted silver-green

Oxalis adenophylla

leaves and lilac-pink, five-petalled flowers 1 in. across, borne freely May to July. *O. enneaphylla*, Patagonia and the Falkland Isles, has a slender rhizomatous root, grey-green leaves, and waxy-white scented flowers. Mexico provides bulbous-rooted *O. deppei* with rather large roundish leaves and coppery-pink flowers, May to June; and *O. lasiandra*, many-leafleted leaves and purple-crimson flowers in umbles on 12-in. stalks in summer. From South Africa *O. purpurata* var. *bowiei* with shamrock-like leaves has umbels of large purple flowers on stems up to 12 in. tall in August and September. Potted in February-March, JIP No. 2 compost, just below the surface, in pans, plants need only cool growing conditions (50° to 55°F (10° to 13°C)), in cold frame or cool room until growing freely; then they need regular watering, and light, airy conditions in order to flower. After flowering, watering is reduced, and when leaves wither plants are kept dry, stored in a frostproof place until re-potted for another season. Propagate by offsets when re-potting.

Screw Pine
Family PANDANACEAE

Pandanus

These tropical ever-green shrubs and trees make good foliage plants for the house, with long, linear leaves, spirally arranged on their stems, thus inviting the name of Screw Pines. Tree-like in nature, they make only dwarfed plants when pot-grown. *P. veitchii* of Polynesia with drooping, spine-edged leaves of dark green, bordered silver-white, up to 2 ft long, is the common Screw Pine; *P. candelabrum*,

Pandanus veitchii

the Chandelier tree of West Africa, is usually grown in its var. *variegatum* with narrow leaves of bright green with white stripes and white spines, 3 to 6 ft long, which makes an effective pedestal plant; and *P. sanderi*, of Timor, has leaves striped yellow and green, with minute spines, 18 to 24 in. long, and makes a useful compact plant. Potted in February to April, in small pots, JIP No. 3 compost, plants go three or four years without needing re-potting. They welcome sunny positions, well ventilated and moist, with provision for this in a pebbled saucer, free watering and spraying during active summer growth, but much less in winter, and a winter temperature of not less than 55°F (13°C). Propagate by suckers from around the base of plants in spring, bottom heat 65°F (18°C).

Geranium: Stork's Bill

Pelargonium

Family GERANIACEAE

This genus of plants originates in warm temperate regions. The most popular class consists of the Zonal Pelargoniums, called Geraniums. They embrace Zonal, with a darker green horseshoe zone on the leaves, and Variegated forms, with dwarf varieties. Of the Zonals, 'Gustav Emich', semi-double vermilion; 'King of Demark', semi-double salmon - pink; 'Ryecroft White',semi-doublewhite; and 'Paul Crampel', single vermilion, are favourites; and of the variegated-

Pelargonium zonale

leaved, 'Mrs Henry Cox', single, orange-red flower, black, red, green and cream leaf; and 'Mrs Strang', double vermilion flowers, geranium-lake, black, yellow and green leaves. Plants need a standard compost, JIP No. 2 or No. 3 with light, airy conditions, some shade from sun when flowering, regular watering in summer with fortnightly feeding, temperatures of 60° to 65°F (15·5° to 18°C); very moderate watering in winter, minimum temperatures of 50° to 55°F (10° to 13°C) for flowering plants; 45°F (7°C) and almost dry conditions for resting plants. Propagate by cuttings—firm, non-flowered—shoots, 2 to 4 in. long, dried off for twenty-four hours before inserting in JIS compost, with slight heat, 55° to 60°F (13° to 15·5°C). Take in August-September for flowering the following summer; in February-March for winter flowering.

Ivy-leaved Geranium

Family GERANIACEAE

Pelargonium

Pelargonium peltatum 'L'Elégante'

This group of Pelargoniums stems largely from the species *P. peltatum*, a native of South Africa, of shrubby character, with rather weak, straggling branches and shoots, up to 3 ft long, furnished with alternative, five-angular lobed ivy-shaped, somewhat fleshy, green leaves, 2 to 3 in. across, and carmine-rose heads of flowers on 3- to 4-in. stalks from the leaf axils in summer. There are several selected forms, of which 'L'Elégante', with single, white, purple-feathered flowers; 'Mme Crousse', pale pink, double flowers; 'Abel Carriere', double, Tyrian purple; 'Galilee', double, rose pink; and 'Mrs W. A. R. Clifton', double, scarlet; and the hybrid 'Millfield Gem', double, fuchsia purple, and white, are well-favoured. They make choice plants for pedestals with branches hanging, or may be used as short climbers with trellis support, or by judicious pinching out of growing points, kept more compact. Cutural needs are similar to those of the Zonal Pelargoniums(q.v.) grown to flower in summer. Flowered plants may be cut hard back in March. Propagate by cuttings in August-September, as for Zonal Pelargoniums.

Pelargonium

Show Pelargoniums are divided into Regal and Fancy, and are largely hybrid, flowering in late spring and summer. They all tend to have crinkled, green leaves, toothed at the edges. The Regals have strong branching growth. Fancy Pelargoniums are more compact with smaller, prettily marked flowers. Of Regals 'Carisbrooke', single, rose-pink, fringed flowers; 'Lady Torsden', single, cherry-madder; 'Lord Bute', dark purple; 'Grand Slam', red and carmine,

Pelargonium domesticum

are pleasing; and of Fancy, 'Sanchoe Panza', purple; 'Rose of Bengal', lavender with maroon marking; and 'Catford Belle', pink, may be cited. Show Pelargoniums need good light, airy conditions, and cool temperatures; watering should be liberal from March to June, and then moderated. After flowering, plants may be allowed to dry off for two to three weeks; in early August all shoots are cut back to one or two joints; and when new growth begins the plants should be repotted, JIP No. 3 compost, firmly, and kept under light, cool conditions, watered only sparingly. By January, they may be potted into larger pots. Winter temperature of about 45° to 50°F (7° to 10°C). Propagate by cuttings of ripened shoots in July-August, bottom heat of 65°F (15·5°C).

149

Peperomia

Family PIPERACEAE

Peperomia hederifolia

Of 400 species of herbs from South America and tropical regions, some of the more decorative are: *P. argyreia* (syn. *P. sandersii*), Brazil, producing orb-shaped leaves of fleshy texture on dark red stalks; *P. caperata*, dwarfish, with oval, tapering leaves of dark, ribbed, green leaves, greyish-green along the ribs, and white, taper-like spikes of flowers in season; *P. hederifolia* with larger cordate leaves and fewer flowers; *P. marmorata* with ovate, fleshy leaves of rich bright green, marbled white, with many white upright flower spikes; and *P. magnoliaefolia* shrub-like, with oval, long leaves, olive green, marked with lighter stripes, in its var. *variegata*. Of trailing habit are *P. glabella*, with roundish, taper-pointed, glossy-green leaves on red stems; and *P. serpens* (syn. *scandens*) var. *variegata*, with cream-margined, pale green ovalish leaves. A compost as for *Aechmea* (q.v.) suits admirably. Light, airy conditions without draughts, only moderate watering, even more sparing in winter, and minimum temperature of 50° to 55°F (10° to 13°C) suit these plants best. Propagate by cuttings: of leaves, inserting their stalks in the rooting medium; of stems in the case of trailing varieties, in spring and summer, bottom heat of 60°F (15·5°C).

Philodendron

Family ARACEAE

Philodendron

This genus of tropical American climbing shrubs is grown for its magnificent foliage. The more easily grown include *P. scandens* of Vera Cruz and Panama, of twining habit, with dark green, heart-shaped, pointed leaves, reddish beneath; *P. bipinnatifidum*, Brazil, short-stemmed with bright green, deeply divided leaves; *P. elegans*, an erect climber with large, deeply lobed leaves,

Philodendron melanochryson

palm-like in effect; *P. islemanni*, erect, slow growing, with aerial roots and beautiful arrow-shaped leaves; *P. melanochryson*, an erect slim climber of Brazil, with heart-shaped, dark-green leaves with velvety, golden sheen; and *P. verrucosum*, Ecuador, erect growing, with beautiful, heart-shaped leaves. Potted in February to April, compost as for *Maranta* (q.v.), they do excellently trained up a cylinder or bark or a support of sphagnum moss tied fairly thickly around a stout stake, and kept moist for the benefit of the aerial roots. All Philodendrons are best in shade, out of draughts, and need adequate watering at all times, with spraying to promote humidity in dry atmospheres; winter minimum temperature of 55°F (13°C) is essential. Propagate by cuttings of stems in JIC, bottom heat of 75°F (23°C).

151

Artillery Plant: Stingless Nettle

Family URTICACEAE

Pila

Pilea cadierei

A genus of the Nettle family, *Pilea* contains only a few species which are house-grown. The chief is *P. cadierei*, a bushy perennial introduced to France from Indo-China in 1938, and since vegetatively propagated to spread over Europe and America from the type-plant. It grows about 10 in. high, with long-stalked, oblong ovate leaves, sharply pointed and shallowly toothed, $2\frac{1}{2}$ in. to $3\frac{1}{2}$ in. long, half as wide, strongly three-nerved and dark green, with conspicuous silver-green patches between the veins. *P. spruceana* of Peru and Venezuela is dwarf and less showy, with leaves in opposite double pairs, ovate, hairy and bronzy-green, but produces small nettle-like, greenish flowers in crowded racemes from the leaf axils freely. *P. microphylla* (*P. mucosa*), a freely-branching dwarf plant of 6 in. with tiny leaves, of tropical America, has tiny inconspicuous flowers which give off clouds of pollen when flicked or shaken and has long been known as the Artillery Plant, Gunpowder Plant or Pistol Plant. A compost of JIP No. 2 suits these plants, and light, airy growing conditions, with regular watering and feeding in summer; only moderate watering in winter with minimum temperature of 55°F (13°C). Propagate by cuttings of stems, or division.

Cape Leadwort

Plumbago

Family PLUMBAGINACEAE

At one time reputed as a remedy for lead poisoning, the Plumbago or Leadworts are now seen as a genus of some ten species of annuals, perennials and shrubs, found in the warmer regions of the world. The one chiefly grown as a house plant is *P. capensis*, a lovely climbing South African shrub of 3 to 9 ft when pot-grown, with alternate, oblongish leaves of about 2 in. and spikes of beautiful pale blue flowers with long corollas, produced more or less on one side freely

Plumbago capensis

in summer; and there is a good white-flowering variety *alba*. Plants may be potted in March, JIP No. 3 compost, and grown in light, airy conditions, temperatures of 55° to 65°F (13° to 18°C), watering freely to September. After flowering, the flowered shoots are pruned back to within about 1 in. of their base, as flowers are produced on the new shoots of the current year's growth each year. From then on the plant needs little water and while leafless, should be kept with a minimum temperature of 45°F (7°C) in a cool greenhouse or plant room. Propagate by seeds in spring, 70°F (23°C) bottom heat; or by cuttings of side shoots in spring or early summer, from which a flowering succession of plants can be grown.

153

Shield Fern: Wood Fern

Family POLYPODIACEAE   *Polystichum*

Polystichum acrostichoides

Free-growing and easily managed, there are several ferns of this genus that make pleasing evergreen foliage plants. *P. acrostichoides* of North America has fronds of 1 to 2 ft with narrow, finely serrated pinnae which in its var. *incisum* are acutely pointed; in var. *grandiceps* the tips are well-crested. In *P. adiantiforme* (syn.) *P. capense*), found in countries as far apart as South Africa, New Zealand and South America, the fronds grow up to 3 ft long, 1 to 1½ ft wide. *P. aristatum* is spread from the Himalayas, through China and Japan to Australia, and forms a pleasing fern with fronds of 1 to 2 ft long, 9 to 12 in. broad, much divided pinnately, with pinnules having awned teeth. For heavily shaded, cool rooms, the native *P. lonchitis*, or Holly Fern, is well suited, with its pinnate fronds of up to 2 ft long and 2 to 3 in. broad. Potted in March, a simple compost of equal parts by volume sandy loam, fibrous peat and a little charcoal is suitable, and they succeed best in shady quarters, with free watering in summer, only moderate in winter, and winter temperatures of 50° to 55°F (10° to 13°C). Propagate by division of crowns in spring, or by spores, sown on surface of above compost, when available.

Primula

Family PRIMULACEAE

The Primrose genus is of over 500 species. Of interest for house decoration are the Malacoides, Obconica and Sinenses. *P. malacoides*, collected in Yunnan, is the Fairy Primrose with a scape of 8 to 10 in. bearing mauve flowers in whorls up its length, from a rosette of basal, broad oblong to ovate, shallowly lobed and stalked leaves in winter. Cultivation has led to improved forms, larger flowers, and larger range of colours in named var-

Primula malacoides

ieties. *P. obconica*, a related species from Ichang, China, has pale lilac or purplish, yellow-eyed flowers, borne in umbels on scapes of 6 to 8 in. in winter; preference is now given to a race of very large flowering *gigantea* in blue, lilac, rose and salmon strains. These Primulas need light, airy conditions, with winter temperatures of 50°F (10°C) to 55°F (13°C), with moderate watering. They are perennial and may be grown on. New plants may be propagated by seeds sown in JIS compost in May, temperature 60°F (15·5°C), pricked-off early into pans, and then in about three weeks into 3 in. pots JIP No. 2 and grown in cold greenhouse or frame until September, with a move into 4½- to 6-in. pots. Plants may also be divided in spring when re-potting.

Chinese Primrose

Family PRIMULACEAE *Primula*

Primula sinensis

The Chinese Primrose, *P. sinensis*, was cultivated by the Chinese for centuries prior to its western introduction in 1820. It bears purplish-rose, yellow-eyed flowers in whorls of six to ten on scapes rising up to 6 in. from broadly ovate, lobed leaves, covered with a soft down and often reddish beneath, in winter and spring. Through improvement and selection, a most colourful and decorative range of single- and double-flowering, and Giant hybrid strains has been evolved; typical of which are 'Dazzler', mandarin red; 'His Excellency', vermilion; 'Pink Enchantress', rose and salmon; 'Reading Blue', royal blue; 'Royal White', and 'Scarlet King', all single flowering; and 'Double Charm', salmon pink; 'Double Dazzler', mandarin red; 'Double Queen of Pinks'; and 'Double Purity', white, all double-flowering. The variety *stellata* with tall, graceful branching flower stems and tiers of starry flowers, has also undergone transformation in colour range and form, and named strains of merit include 'Beacon Star', orange-scarlet and salmon; 'Enchantress', salmon-pink; 'Fire King', crimson; 'Gaiety', pink; 'Giant Orange Glow Star', orange-salmon; 'Light Blue Star' and 'Giant White Star'. Culture is as for *P. malacoides* and *P. obconica* (q.v.).

Rebutia

Family CATACEAE

From Argentina and
Bolivia, these cacti
provide freely flower-
ing plants for house
culture. They are
largely small, low-
growing rounded
plants without ribs
but with small tuber-
cles or warts, spirally

Rebutia miniscula

arranged, and small spines; the red, orange or yellow,
funnel-shaped, comparatively large flowers are produced from areoles at the sides and base of the plants,
even when very small and young. *R. fiebrigii* is notable
for its long, white, bristle-like numerous spines, and
has orange-red flowers with white stamens. *R. miniscula*,
a tiny globular plant with very small spines, bears red
flowers, ringing it at the base; *R. pseudodeminuta* and
R. deminuta are somewhat similar, the former having
longer spines and golden-orange flowers round the
base, and the latter large bright red flowers. *R. senilis*
has rounded bodies covered with long, white bristle
spines, and red flowers; and a var. *violaciflora* with
violet flowers; *R. steinmannii* forms a small, oblong
plant with short spines and flowers in shades of red.
Grown in a porous compost, these plants are happy in
light shade with plenty of water from spring to autumn,
but little in winter, and a minimum temperature of
50°F (10°C). Propagate by offsets in March, or by seeds
which germinate readily, temperature 65°F (18°C).

Kurume Azalea

Family ERICACEAE

Rhododendron

Of Rhododendron genus, the Azalea series makes most decorative house plants, especially varieties from Japan under the name of 'Kurume' Azaleas. These are more or less evergreen shrubs, developed from such species as *R. obtusum*. Pot-grown, they make pleasing bushy plants with their small green ovate leaves, and flower freely through winter and early spring. Varieties are many, but

Rhododendron obtusum

favourites include 'Beni-giri', red flowers; 'Blaauw's Pink', double; 'Christmas Cheer', red; 'Hinodigiri', bright red; 'Hinomanyo', salmon-pink; 'Mother's Day', salmon-red; and 'White Lady', white. There are also large-flowering kinds such as 'Alice', salmon-red; 'Orange Beauty'; 'Palestrina', white; 'Schubert', bright pink; and 'Vuyk's Scarlet'. Plants require potting in lime-free compost, such as the JI Rhododendron mixture, and light, airy and cool conditions, with moderate watering and a winter temperature of 45° to 55°F (7° to 13°C). They benefit from being sprayed on warm days; by June, the plants may stand out of doors in warm, wind-sheltered positions, with roots cool and well watered, being brought in again in October–November. Propagate by cuttings of half-ripe shoots taken with a 'heel' in spring, under glass, bottom heat 60°F (15·5°C).

Indian Azalea

Rhododendron

Family ERICACEAE

This group of ever-green shrubs is commonly listed under *Azalea indicum* and the plants are known as Indian Azaleas, though their origin lies with a Chinese species, *Rhododendron simsii*, from which the now many varieties of varying flower colour and form are developed. These are sold to flower in the house during winter and early spring and make very pleasing bushy shrubs. Varie-

Rhododendron simsii var.
'Perle de Noisy'

ties are legion, particularly semi-double or double-flowering. Typical named sorts are: early-flowering—'Beatrice', orange-red; 'Kees Bier', red; 'Perle de Noisy' salmon and white; 'Petrick Alba', white; mid-season (new year) flowering—'Eclaireur', red; 'Pink Pearl'; 'Hollandia', orange; 'Vervaeneana' in pink, salmon-pink and brick-red forms; late (early spring) flowering—'Hexe', red; 'Madame J. Haerens', pink; and 'Niobe', white. A lime-free compost is essential; moderate watering in winter, with temperatures of 50° to 60°F (10° to 15·5°C), water more freely after March; prune straggly growths and remove spent flowers only, and in June stand out of doors as for 'Kurume' Azaleas, until October-November. Re-pot, when needed, directly after flowering. Propagate by firm cuttings of heeled shoots in summer.

Boat Lily
Family COMMELINACEAE

Rhoeo

Rhoeo discolor

The sole species in this genus, *R. discolor*, is a rather striking and distinctive perennial herb, nearly related to *Tradescantia*, and found in Central American countries from Florida to below Mexico. It grows upright with a thick, fleshy stem, from which broad, linear, thick-bladed and pointed leaves, 6 to 9 in. long, are produced in rosetted formation, olive green, sometimes more lightly striped, and purplish beneath. The flowers are white or blue, and quite tiny, being formed at the base of the leaves in curious boat-shaped involucres of overlapping bracts at various times of the year. Its var. *vittata* has leaves striped lengthwise in a creamy-yellow. This unusual plant is not hard to grow, potted in February to April, JIP No. 2 compost, and given partial shade, good ventilation and fairly liberal watering, March to October, and more moderate watering thereafter, with a minimum winter temperature of about 50°F (10°C). Propagate by young cuttings of offshoots from near the base of the stem, spring and summer, 60°F (15·5°C).

Grape Ivy

Rhoicissus

Family VITACEAE

Although of the Vine family, the eight species of this genus are more properly described as branching climbing shrubs akin to *Cissus*. Only one, *R. rhomboidea*, native of Natal, is commonly cultivated; a moderate, erect climber for pots, given a cane support, with rhomboid, toothed leaves, long-stalked, and three-leafleted, of glossy, dark olive green, and the growing tips coloured brownish-pink. It grows rapidly, but the flowers which may appear in tendril-bearing cymes on mature plants are negligible, though giving way to very tiny, grape-like berries which are edible. Cultivation is like that given for *Cissus* (q.v.).

Rhoicissus rhomboidea

Rochea

Family CRASSULACEAE

Rochea falcata

This small genus of four species of succulents from South Africa provides some bright and pretty early summer-flowering shrubs for the house. *R. coccinea* (syn. *Crassula coccinea,Kalosanthes coccinea*) grows about 1 ft high, with stems crowded with small green leathery leaves in four ranks, and terminating in showy clusters of tubular scarlet flowers throughout July. *R. jasminea* is of prostrate habit, with white, turning pink, flowers in April-May; while *R. versicolor* grows erectly with 12-in. stems, and bears flowers which may be white, pink and yellow and sometimes scarlet without, in May-June. *R. falcata* (syn. *Crassula falcata*) grows erectly,with 8-in. stems, crowded with fleshy leaves, and topped with red clustered flowers in summer. Hybrids and varieties of these plants are sometimes offered. Their culture calls for potting in JIP composts, in March; free watering in active growth until August, more moderate watering until about November, and very little in winter, when a minimum temperature of about 50°F (10°C) is preferable. Propagate by cuttings of shoots, about 3 in. long, taken in late spring or summer, dried and inserted in JIP No. 1, and given good light.

African Violet

Saintpaulia

Family GESNERIACEAE

Saintpaulia ionantha

S. ionantha, called the African or Usambara Violet, from some resemblance of its growth habit and flowers to those of Violets, was introduced in 1893 from eastern tropical Africa. The leaves are broadly oval and pointed darkish green and somewhat hairy, spreading flatly to form the background for violet-blue flowers, with a centre of orange-yellow stamens, in loose cymes on stalks. There are many varieties, in shades of blue, purple, pink, white and almost red, and single- and double-flowering forms. To do well, plants need to be in small pots, about 3 in. at first, with a move to 4 in. only when plants are really large in early spring; JIP No. 3 compost is suitable, with a little extra sifted leaf-mould and crushed charcoal. Plenty of sun and light are needed, with humidity and warmth. Plants are best stood on saucers full of pebbles, kept wet, and watering should be done to keep the soil moist, using water of room temperature. Plants may be mist-sprayed on dry days. Temperatures tolerated range between 50° and 80°F (10° and 26·5 °C), but a drop below 60°F (15·5°C) checks flowering. Propagate by stalked leaves, inserting the stalks in moist sand, vermiculite or JIC compost, with close atmosphere; or in water, temperature 70°F (21°C); by seeds in spring.

163

Sansevieria

Family HAEMODORACEAE

Sansevieria

Sansevieria trifasciata

From the fifty species or so of these rhizomatous-rooted tropical perennials, only a few are cultivated, chiefly for their very attractive, beautifully marked, tough, fleshy leaves, growing stiffly upright on very short stems from the soil. The most popular is *S. trifasciata* var. *laurentii*, sometimes called Snake Plant, or more unkindly Mother-in-law's Tongue, from western tropical Africa. It throws up sword-like, pointed leaves, coloured in various banded shades of green and outlined close to the margins with stripes of golden yellow, 12 to 36 in. tall. Only one or two new leaves are made each year, and flowering is rare, though the racemes of pale greenish-white flowers on tall stems are quite pretty. *S. cylindrica* has arching, 1-in.-thick rounded leaves in light and dark greens, up to 3 ft long, and *S. hahnii* broad, pointed leaves in rosette formation, irregularly marked greyish and dark green. Sometimes called Cast-iron Plants for their tolerance of house conditions, these plants grow well in light or shade, in a temperature range of 50° to 80°F (10° to 26·50°C), but should not be over-watered.

Mother of Thousands

Saxifraga

Family SAXIFRAGACEAE

This large genus of over 300 species of perennial herbs is best represented in the house by *S. stolonifera* (syn. *S. sarmentosa*), a native of China and Japan, introduced in 1815, and long esteemed as a window plant. It makes a tufted plant, with long-stalked, broad-bladed, round leaves, marbled white along the veins, branching flower stems, carrying white, yellow-centred and red-spotted flowers in July and August; it has a habit of forming numerous creeping red-stalked stolons or runners bearing young plantlets, which has earned it several sobriquets such as 'Mother of Thousands', 'Roving Sailor', 'Aaron's Beard' and 'Strawberry Geranium'.

Saxifraga stolonifera

Its var. *tricolor* makes a smaller plant with leaves deeply cut and irregularly marked red, cream and green, and is somewhat more tender and less free in producing stolons, but a very attractive plant. Potted in JIP No. 2 compost in March, plants are happy in light, airy conditions, with free watering in the summer and very moderate in winter, with a minimum temperature of 50°F (10°C). Propagate by pegging the plantlets in small pots of compost, severing when rooted.

Schefflera

Family ARALIACEAE

Schefflera

The plants of this genus number about 150 species of tall shrubs or trees found in the tropics, but few are known in cultivation. An Australian species, *S. actinophylla*, has proved most promising for house culture; its upright thick stem has spreading leafleted leaves on firm, wiry stalks growing alternately from it. The leaflets are of long oval shape, glossy green, lightening at the veins, and number three on the early first leaves, but five to seven on older leaves produced as the plant ages, when it may produce panicles of small greenish flowers from the axils of the leaves. Potted in JIP No. 3 compost in March, a plant needs very good light, airy conditions, with free watering during April to October, then only very moderate watering in winter, with minimum temperature of 50°F (10°C). Propagation may be attempted by stem cuttings in spring, with bottom heat of 65°F (15·5C).

Schefflera actinophylla

Schizocentron

Schizocentron

Family MELASTOMATACEAE

S. elegans (syn. *Heeria elegans*) is a low creeping herbaceous plant of Mexico, sole representative of its genus, which forms a dense mat of branching stems, rooting at the leaf nodes as they go, with small, opposite, broadly ovate leaves, becoming almost covered with deep purple, four-petalled flowers, borne at the ends of short shoots throughout May and June It makes a striking and pleasing picture if grown in a fairly large pan, or

Schizocentron elegans

it is adaptable to growing on the surface of large pots containing palms or similar tall plants. It succeeds well in JIP No. 3 compost, and grows under light, airy and warm conditions; it needs to be watered well when in active growth, very moderately in winter, minimum temperature of about 50°F (10°C). Propagate by pieces of rooted stem taken from the plant in spring or early summer, or by seed, with bottom heat of 65°F (18°C), in spring.

Scindapsus

Family ARACEAE

Scindapsus

Scindapsus pictus

Of the Arum family, the climbing plants in cultivation as house plants are: *S. aureus* of the Solomon Isles, a branching climber, which can be trained up a cane but is better up a cylinder of bark or one of wire-mesh netting filled with sphagnum moss. The thin, leathery leaves are stalked, heart-shaped at the base and ovate, growing larger as a plant becomes older, with a bright green basic colouring, broken with irregular marbling and spotting in yellow.

'Marble Queen' is a slower-growing form with dark green leaves, heavily variegated in creamy-white; and 'Golden Queen' has leaves almost wholly coloured golden yellow. *S. pictus* var. *argyraeus*, of Malaya and Java, known as the Silver Vine, since its 2-in., heart-shaped dark green leaves are marked with silver spots, growing alternately from a slender main stem, makes an effective climber of many feet, if unchecked. It is, however, now held to be the juvenile form of *S. pictus*, rather than a variety, and as it grows and matures, the leaves become bigger and the silvering disappears. These plants are managed much as Philodendrons, with partial shade, draught-free position, moderate watering, provision for humidity and even temperatures, preferably 50° to 60°F (10° to 15.5°C) in winter. Propagate by stem cuttings.

Club Rush

Scirpus

Family CYPERACEAE

This is really a genus of about 200 species of hardy marsh plants for out of doors, but one of them, the native Club Rush— *S. riparius* (syn.) *S. cernuus, S. gracilis, Isolepis gracilis* — is almost invariably cultivated as a pot plant. In nature it occurs in places as wide apart as Siberia and South Africa, as well as Western Europe and the Mediterranean regions, and makes a pretty evergreen of

Scirpus riparius

close-tufted habit, with pendent grass-like leaves, up to 12 in. long, with yellowish-brown and purple-tinged basal sheaths. It requires a moist compost of two parts by volume loam, two parts leaf-mould or peat and one part sand, with a little charcoal, and may be potted in March, to grow in good light, with frequent watering in summer, moderate watering in winter, and a minimum temperature of about 50°F (10°C). Propagate by division in March.

Stonecrop

Family CRASSULACEAE *Sedum*

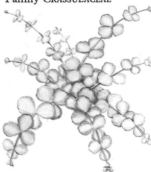

Sedum sieboldii

Of this large genus of succulent plants, one of the most satisfactory, in that it will tolerate a certain amount of neglect, is *S. sieboldii* of Japan, which grows with low, arching stems, beset with rounded leaves in whorls of three, somewhat fleshy, blue-green and often edged red or pink in autumn, when large umbelliferous heads of pinkish flowers are borne at the ends of the stems. It dies down in winter, but the budding of new shoots is soon in evidence, and they grow apace from February onwards. The var. *medio-variegatum* has leaves with a yellow centre. Others are *S. morganianum*, with long hanging stems, clothed in whitish-green, overlapping, 1-in., lance-shaped leaves, and terminal heads of reddish flowers, apt to drip nectar freely; and *S. stahlii*, with erect and spreading stems of 4 to 8 in., clothed in egg-shaped, small leaves and lovely cymes of yellow flowers in autumn. They are natives of Mexico, and more or less evergreen. Potted in March-April, JIP No. 1 compost, they welcome sun and good light, with moderate watering at first, then more liberal in summer, but very little water should be given in winter, with minimum temperature of 50°F (10°C). Propagate by division in March.

Gloxinia

Sinningia

Family GESNERIACEAE

Native to Brazil, it is from *S. speciosa* that the plants known as 'Gloxinias', have been developed. Exceptional strains of these beautiful and decorative flowering plants have been raised, with flowers borne more erectly, extremely solid and flaring wide at the mouth, with a colour range of pure white to deep crimson, in selfs, in forms spotted or laced with another colour, or with contrasting margins. Specialist growers' lists should be consulted

Sinningia speciosa

for named forms and hybrids. With proper care, plants can be kept in cultivation for many years. From seeds, Gloxinias can be flowered in about six months. Tubers are potted in February, JIP No. 3 compost, one to a 4½-in. pot, temperature 60° to 65°F (15.5° to 18°C), to grow in shade, keeping just moist until growth is well forward, and increasing watering when roots are well formed; move to 6-in. pots when buds are forming, with weekly feeding to supplement watering. No water should lodge on the crowns or leaves, however. Plants flower from June to autumn. After flowering, withhold water gradually, dry off the tubers and store in the dark in frostproof room or cupboard or attic, temperature 50°F (10°C). Propagate by seeds, bottom heat 70°F (21°C), January to March; by leaf cuttings in summer, in propagating case.

Solanum

Family SOLANACEAE

Solanum

Solanum capsicastrum

Of this large genus, the most popular as pot plants for the house are the shrubs *S. capsicastrum* of Brazil, known as the Winter Cherry, which grows 1 to 2 ft high, with twin lance-shaped leaves, one smaller than the other, and small white flowers, followed by scarlet, cherry-like fruits; and *S. pseudocapsicum* of Madeira, taller-growing, with more oblong, lance-shaped leaves, similar white flowers followed by red, showy fruits. There are several good forms of each species; hybrids such as *Weatherillii* are distinctive for oval-pointed fruits. The plants are grown for their coloured fruits from mid-November onwards, and may be bought from a nursery or raised from seeds. Winter care calls for ample light and sun, airy but draughtless conditions, frequent watering in dry atmospheres, with spraying of foliage on sunny days. Hot and too dry conditions will cause berry- and leaf-fall. After fruiting, shoots can be pruned back hard and when new growth appears, plants re-potted and grown on again under cool conditions in greenhouse or frame, or out of doors in June, until fruiting. Propagate by seeds in JIS compost, January-March, temperature 65°F (18°C); by cuttings of shoots in spring, bottom heat of 65°F (18°C).

Sparmannia   Family TILIACEAE

There are about four species to this genus of the Lime or Linden family, native to South Africa. The one chiefly cultivated is *S. africana*, known as African Hemp, and often as the indoor Linden tree, and although introduced in 1790 is still too seldom seen. Of easy culture it grows very rapidly, and while it will make a specimen of 10 ft, it may be kept much smaller by pruning. With its evergreen foliage of large, lime-green, hairy, heart-shaped, slender-pointed and well-veined

Sparmannia africana

leaves, up to 6 in. long and 4 in. wide, it always has a restful quality about it, and the flowers are borne in stalked profusion in umbels, four-parted and white, with a centre brush of yellow filaments, purple tipped, in late summer to early winter. Potted in March-April, JIP No. 3 compost, in 6-in. or larger pots, plants are best placed out of doors in June, in warm, sheltered position, pots sunk to their rims in the soil, and kept well watered and sprayed; in October they are brought into light cool, airy conditions, temperature 50° to 55°F (10° to 13°C), and watered moderately being pruned as hard as necessary in February. Propagate by cuttings of young, or one-year-old shoots in March-April, with heat of about 55° to 60°F (13° to 15·5°C).

173

Peace Lily

Family ARACEAE

Spathiphyllum

Spathiphyllum wallisii

This genus of Aroids contains some twenty-seven species of stemless, evergreen herbs, chiefly found in tropical America. The most attractive for the house is probably *S. wallisii*, native of Columbia, which grows with broad, lance-shaped, glossy bright green, well-stalked leaves, up to 9 in. long and with fine regular veins; from among these arises an erect flower stem carrying a spathe that turns white, and a spadix, densely flowered, in summer. A compariot, *S. patinii*, is similarly white-flowering, but larger in all its parts. These plants grow quickly, need a shady position, with provision for humidity and temperatures of 75° to 80°F (23° to 26·5°C) in summer and not less than 65°F (18°C) in winter, with copious watering, frequent feeding and spraying in summer, moderate watering in winter. Re-potting is usually necessary annually in March, JIP No. 3 compost. Propagate by division when re-potting.

Cape Primrose

Streptocarpus

Family GESNERIACEAE

Horticultural interest in this genus centres around the hybrid Cape Primroses, resulting from the crossing of South African species, notably *S. rexii*, with others such as *S. saundersii*, *S. dunnii*, *S. parviflorus*, *S. cyaneus*, *S. wendlandii* and *S. woodii*, with the evolution of a magnificent race of fine flowering plants grouped under × *S. hybridus*. They are stemless, with large rich green leaves of a texture and shape resembling those of the Primrose, and bear bell-

Streptocarpus × hybridus

shaped, gloxinia-like flowers on stout stems in a range of shades of purple, white, blue, violet, red, rose and pink, often beautifully marked, and they flower through summer and autumn. Specialist growers offer their own strains of giant-flowered hybrids. Plants may be brought in during summer, given light, airy positions, shaded from direct hot sun, and liberal watering to October, with weekly feeding when in flower; after flowering watering is reduced to the point of keeping the plants almost dry in winter, with a minimum temperature of 45°F (7°C). Re-pot in March, JIP No. 3 compost. Propagate by leaf cuttings in summer, division of old plants in March; or raise new plants from seeds sown thinly and shallowly, JIS compost, in January to March, with bottom heat of 60°F (15·5°C).

Palm

Family PALMACEAE

Syagrus

Syagrus weddeliana

This genus of South American Palm contains about twelve species, closely related to *Cocos* and formerly included in it. The one chiefly grown for house decoration is *S. weddeliana* (syn. *Cocos weddeliana*), accounted by many as the most elegant and graceful of all palms and much valued for table decoration when young. With slender stem, netted with black fibres, and gracefully arching, feathery, pinnatisect, narrow, long pinnae of dark shining green, growing 1 to 4 ft long, this plant lends distinction to a room at all seasons. In the var. *pynaertii*, the pinnae or leaflets are somewhat broader but more tightly packed together. They are usually available in small pots, grow slowly and need plenty of water in the summer months, but moderate watering only at other times, with a minimum winter temperature of about 50°F (10°C). A good sponging of the leaves is needed periodically and plants may be re-potted when root-bound, using JIP No. 2 compost. Propagate by seeds, with bottom heat of 85°F (29°C), under glass.

Syngonium

Syngonium
Family ARACEAE

Of about fourteen species of climbing Aroids, natives of tropical Central and South America, closely related to Philodendron, only two are in general cultivation. *S. podophyllum*, of Central America, is a pleasing plant grown in its var. *albolineatum*, of twining growth with slim stems, rather exaggerated arrow - head - shaped, triangular leaves, up to 7 or 9 in. long and pleasantly variegated pale green along the mid-ribs and veins, on a dark green ground, and aerial roots. Estab-

Syngonium vellozianum

lished plants may produce flowers within a rose-coloured spathe. *S. vellozianum* of Brazil branches freely, with tri-lobed large leaves, made up of a broad, lance-shaped centre lobe and two flanking, smaller, spear-shaped lobes, which are pleasing in shape and glossy green. Pot in February-March, compost as for *Maranta* (q.v.). These climbers do best of all on cylinders of bark, or supports of moist sphagnum moss, wired to a stake or strong tube of wire-mesh, in partial shade, out of draughts, and in even temperatures: 55° to 65°F (13° to 18°C) in winter, with adequate watering at all times and provision for humidity. Propagate by stem cuttings, though rather high temperatures are needed, 75° to 85°F (23° to 29°C).

Spider-flower

Family MELASTOMATACEAE

Tibouchina

Tibouchina semidecandra

A native of the forests of Southern Brazil, *T. semidecandra* var. *floribunda* is one of the finest evergreen shrubs for indoor culture and belongs to a genus of about 150 species found in tropical Southern America. It is an evergreen shrub with squarish stems, large, silky ovate leaves, 3 to 6 in. long, strongly ribbed or nerved longitudinally in pairs, and royal purple, velvety-textured flowers, 3 to 5 in. across, borne freely at the ends of shoots in three-forked panicles in late summer or autumn. Even small, young plants flower freely, and although capable of growing to 10 ft or more eventually, this plant should not be dismissed on account of its potential bigness. Potted in March, JIP No. 3 compost, plants benefit by being placed in sunny positions in a plant room or large window, liberally watered from April to September, more moderately at other times, and a winter minimum temperature of 50°F (10°C). Plants may be pruned into shape each February and should be re-potted before being allowed to become pot-bound. Propagate by cuttings of firm side shoots, spring or summer, with bottom heat of 75°F (23°C).

Tolmiea

The single species of this genus, *T. menziesii*, is a herbaceous perennial with a creeping rhizomatous rootstock, native to North-west America, and although virtually hardy, it makes an interesting pot plant for cool rooms and shade on account of its growth habit of making small new plantlets from buds at the junctions of leaf stalks and blades on the older heart-shaped and lobed darkish-green leaves. The leaves are radical and the plant is of tufted habit, of 12 to 24 in. high, with a loose

Tolmiea menziesii

raceme of greenish, nodding flowers at the head of a leafy flower stem in summer. It has several common names, Pig-a-back, Youth-on-Age, and Thousand Mothers being typical. Potted in March, JIP No. 2 compost, a plant needs only cool conditions and will stand shade well, with free watering in summer, when the plant can be stood out of doors for a time, and only very moderate watering in winter, with a minimum temperature of 45°F (7°C). Propagate by detaching plantlets, after layering and rooting in small pots.

Tradescantia

Family COMMELINACEAE

Tradescantia fluminensis

The species that are grown as house plants are creepers or trailers, appreciated for their colourful foliage and easy culture; they come from South America. *T. fluminensis* (syn. *T. fluviatilis*) has narrowly ovate, acutely pointed leaves, apt to vary in colour according to the light, being green in poor light and striped purplish-red in bright light; and there are selected forms in which leaf colour is more pronounced, such as *aurea*, with pale green leaves striped yellow and white; and *variegata*, with leaves pale green, striped silvery-white, when grown in good light. Slightly less hardy, *T. blossfeldiana* trails with thick fleshy, rather hairy stems, furnished with rather leathery, elliptical pointed leaves of dark green, purplish and hairy beneath, up to 3 in. long. These trailing plants are often known as 'Wandering Jew' or 'Wandering Sailor'. Potted almost any time in early spring or summer, plants grow in any reasonably well-drained compost and need only regular watering in summer, moderate in winter, with minimum temperature of 50°F (10°C). As plants become unkempt, stems should be pinched back. *T. blossfeldiana* needs warmer conditions. Propagate by stem cuttings in spring or summer.

Tulipa

Family LILIACEAE

Tulips which lend themselves to pot culture are: Single Early Tulips, Double Early Tulips, Mendel Tulips, and the Triumph, Darwin and Cottage Tulips in several varieties. Some may be obtained specially prepared for early flowering. Their culture is similar to that of Hyacinths (q.v.), the bulbs, after potting, being kept cool and dark until roots are well formed and growth shows above the surface, when they are brought to light, warmth and flowering positions gradually, with judicious watering. Several *Tulipa* species make excellent pot plants for cool rooms

Tulipa kaufmanniana

in February to April, such as *T. greigii*, Turkestan, 8 in., orange-scarlet flowers, and mottled leaves; *T. kaufmanniana*, the Water-lily Tulips, in many varieties, 6 in. with starry flowers; and *T. tarda*, Turkestan, 6 in. with three to five white, yellow-eyed flowers to each stem. These bulbs are planted about four to a 5-in. pot, 3 in. deep, JIP No. 2 compost, in September-November, and placed in cool, dark, conditions until growth is showing, when they are brought to the light and cool room conditions and watered to flower. All tulips should complete their leaf growth after flowering before being lifted and stored. Propagate by offset bulbs.

Periwinkle
Family APOCYNACEAE

Vinca

Vinca rosea

About ten species comprise this genus of perennial herbs and sub-shrubs, which includes the native, hardy trailing Periwinkles; but the one grown as a pot plant is the Madagascar Periwinkle *V. rosea*, a half-hardy, shrubby evergreen of the tropics, which grows about 12 to 18 in. tall, branching, with shining green opposite leaves, and distinctive, showy round flowers opening successively through the spring and summer, white with a red eye in one form, rose-pink in another. It needs regular watering throughout its flowering in a well-lighted, airy position, but only very moderate watering in winter, with a minimum temperature of 55°F (13°C). Pot or re-pot in February-March, JIP No. 3 compost; pinch out the growing points of young new shoots to induce bushiness. Propagate by cuttings of young new shoots in spring in propagating case, temperature 65°F (18°C), or by seeds, bottom heat of 70°F (21°C).

Vriesia

Vriesia   Family BROMELIACEAE

These Bromeliads of Central and South America have rosetted growth of stiff, unarmed, beautifully marbled or banded leaves, and flower stem bearing spikes of showy flowers, colourfully bracted. *V. splendens*, Guinea, is one of the easiest to grow, with stiffish, linear leaves up to 15 in. long and 2½ in. broad, of dullish green, transversely banded brownish-

Vriesia splendens

purple, and a flattish, spear-like flower spike of flaming red bracts, opening to disclose small yellow flowers. *V. carinata* of Brazil is relatively small with its rosette of narrow, sword-like leaves, 6 to 8 in. long and little more than ½ in. wide, an erect flowering scape of about 8 in., with red and yellow keeled bracts and evanescent yellow flowers. *V. saundersii* has a rosette of bluish-green, dotted white, broad linear leaves to about 10 in. long, and a flower scape breaking into a panicle of yellow bracts and long sulphur-yellow flowers about 18 in. tall. A potting compost as for Aechmea (q.v.) is most suitable for these plants, which welcome good light, with moderate watering only, good ventilation and temperatures on the high side, 70°F (21°C) or more in summer, with a winter minimum of 60°F (15·5°C). Propagate by offsets in spring, with bottom heat of 75°F (23°C).

Zebrina

Family COMMELINACEAE

Zebrina pendula

Zebrina

Closely linked to *Trade-scantia*, this genus of trailing or pendulous, branching herbs is native to the Southern States of U.S.A. and Mexico. *Z. pendula* is easily grown, its stems adorned with short-stalked and sheathed, narrowly oval and pointed leaves, beautifully coloured longitudinally with sil-ver and purple to mauve, dark green to the edges, and purplish-red below. The var. *quadricolor* is even more vividly marked, with white, reddish-purple, dark green, and silvery-grey to green. Mauve flowers may be borne in late sum-mer by established plants. *Z. purpusii* is somewhat more delicate, with pendulous habit and slightly smaller leaves than *Z. pendula*, which are dullish green-purple on the surface, more vividly reddish-purple under-neath; clusters of purplish-rose pink flowers may be borne in October. Potted in March, JIP No. 2 compost, these plants should be given good light, airy positions, and be watered freely from March to October, with only moderate watering in winter, with a minimum temperature of 45° to 50°F (7° to 10°C). Shoots may be pinched back in spring or early summer to induce bushiness, and the tip cuttings inserted in JIC compost, for increase, with temperature of about 60°F (15·5°C).

Crab Cactus: Christmas Cactus

Zygocactus
(*Syn. Schlumbergera*)

Family CACTACEAE

Probably one of the most popular and most universally grown cactus in homes, *Z. truncatus* is the sole species of this genus, an epiphytic plant akin to *Epiphyllum* and native to Brazil. With thin, leaf-like, jointed, grey-green pendent stems, it produces during the winter months longish, fuchsia-like flowers, with reflexing petals and protruding long stamens and style, which are a lovely carmine-crimson in the type. There are several varieties in flower colours of white, and different shades of red to cerise, and some flower earlier, others later than Christmas. Potted in compost as for *Epiphyllum* (q.v.), March, plants need partial shade, moderate to free watering until in bud, then rather less, and a short rest after flowering; winter temperature 45° to 50°F (7° to 10°C). Propagate by division or stem cuttings.

Zygocactus truncatus

INDEX

GLOSSARY

Alternate of leaves, arranged in two rows but not opposite; or in spiral arrangements, not more than one at a node.
Annual completing its life cycle within one year from germination.
Anther the part of the stamen which contains the pollen.
Asexual without male or female organs; reproduced without the union of male and female gametes; vegetative reproduction.
Axil angle formed by junction of leaf and stem.
Axillary arising in the axil.

Biennial completing its life-cycle within two years; growing the first year, flowering, fruiting and dying the second.

Genus, Genera a group of species with common structural characteristics.

Glabrous without hairs.

Glaucous bluish.

Gynoecium female part of the flower, comprising the ovary or ovaries with their styles and stigmas.

Half-hardy of exotic plants which require protection from low or freezing temperatures, especially in winter.

Herbaceous of plants, annual, biennial or perennial, which do not form a woody stem; of perennials which die down to the ground or crown annually.

Hermaphrodite containing both stamens and ovary.

Hybrid a plant arising from the fertilization of one species by another.

Inflorescence the flowering branch or portion of the stem above the last leaves, including stalks, bracts and flowers.

Internode the part of stem between two nodes.

Lobed divided by an indentation but not separated.

Monoecious having unisexual flowers, but with both sexes on the same plant.

Node joint; part of stem from which one or more leaves arise.

Obovate inversely ovate, with the broader end terminal.

Orbicular rounded, with equal length and breadth.

Ovate egg-shaped, with broad end nearest the leaf stalk.

Ovary the part of the pistil of a flower enclosing the ovules.

Ovule structure containing the egg, developing into the seed after fertilization.

Palmate divided like a hand, usually of leaves with more than three leaflets arising from a common point.

Panicle a branching racemose inflorescence.

Pedicel the stalk of a single flower.

Peduncle the stalk of an inflorescence or flower-cluster.

Perennial—living for more than two years; normally flowering each year.

Perianth the outer non-essential floral organs, including petals and sepals, when present.

Petiole the stalk of a leaf.

Pinnate—having leaflets arranged in two rows along each side of a common stalk or axis.

Pistil the ovule- and seed-bearing organ, consisting of ovary, stigma and style.

Procumbent lying loosely flat on the surface.

Raceme   a simple, elongated, unbranched inflorescence in which the flowers are borne on pedicels.

Radical   of leaves, arising from the base of the stem, root or rhizome.

Receptacle   the upper part of the stem from which the parts of the flower arise; the torus.

Reflexed   abruptly bent backward or downward.

Rhizome   an underground stem lasting more than one year.

Runner   a special form of stolon, consisting of an aerial branch rooting and forming a new plant at the end.

Rugose   wrinkled.

Saggittate   arrow-shaped, triangular with basal lobes pointing downwards.

Scape   the flowering stem of a plant with all radical leaves, arising from the root.

Sepal   one of the separate green leaves of a calyx.

Serrate   saw-toothed.

Sessile   without a stalk.

Simple   of leaves, not compound.

Species   a group of individuals having the same constant and distinct characters.

Spike   an inflorescence with the flowers sessile along an unbranched axis.

Spore   a small asexual reproductive body, usually a single cell; of fungi, but also of mosses and ferns.

Stamen   the male reproductive organ of a plant, consisting of the filament and pollen-bearing anthers.

Stigma   the receptive surface or part of the pistil which receives the pollen.

Stolon   a creeping stem of short life produced by a plant which has a central rosette or erect stem.

Style   the part of the pistil connecting the ovary and the stigma.

Terminal   borne at the end of a stem or branch.

Tomentum   dense covering of short cottony hairs; adj. tomentose.

Tuber   a swollen portion of a stem or root, produced underground, of one year's duration.

Umbel   an inflorescence in which the flower stalks all arise from the top of the main stem; giving an umbrella-shaped head.

Vein   of leaves, a strand of thick, strengthening and conducting tissue, sometimes called a nerve or rib.

Viscid   sticky.

Whorl   three or more leaves or organs of the same kind arising in a ring at the same level or plane.